THE
COLOR
OF
FASHION

Published in 2022 by Welbeck
an imprint of Welbeck Non-Fiction Limited,
part of Welbeck Publishing Group.
Based in London and Sydney
www.welbeckpublishing.com

A CIP catalogue record for this book is available from the
British Library.

ISBN 978-1-80279-107-5

Printed in Dubai

10 9 8 7 6 5 4 3 2 1

THE COLOR OF FASHION

**The story of clothes
in 10 colors**

CAROLINE YOUNG

WELBECK

Contents

Paris Fashion
Week, 2020

We are living in a time of bold colour choices. A rainbow of hues lights up our Instagram feeds, creating a fantasy world of sun-dappled selfies of influencers dressed in sugar pinks, brilliant blues and tropical greens. Dramatic blocks of colour have also shown their connection to politics, from the white pantsuits worn by members of US Congress that paid tribute to the suffragette movement, to the bright coats worn on a cold January for the 2021 presidential inauguration. National Youth Poet Laureate Amanda Gorman delivered illuminating words while dressed in canary yellow, alongside the new First Lady Jill Biden in sky blue, and Michelle Obama entirely in damson, from her coat to her trousers and sweater.

Introduction

Not only do bright colours stimulate our senses, but we are exposed from a young age to set ideas around the significance of colours in clothing, what meanings they convey and how they make us feel. We often assess a baby's gender depending on whether they're wearing pink or blue, and the fluorescent yellow hi-vis vest warns us of potential danger. Even on the radio, we hear songs where the colour of clothing is connected to a certain emotion, whether it's lust or longing – Bobby Vinton's 'Blue Velvet', The Moody Blues' 'Nights in White Satin', Prince's 'Raspberry Beret', Chris de Burgh's 'Lady in Red', Lana del Rey's 'Blue Jeans'.

There's a long association with red for blood and passion, blue for tranquillity and the endless space between the sea and the sky, and green as the colour of nature. Colour symbolism is often inherited, but it can switch over time, depending on the culture. In the West, Victorian widows may have been shrouded in black, but in India, widows wear white; green may mean good luck in Ireland, but in China, the family members of prostitutes traditionally wear a green hat or headscarf; and while Western brides wear virginal white, in Hinduism, brides wear red as a symbol of prosperity and fertility.

Sometimes we make assumptions about the colours people wear, either from our own experience or from stereotypes we have learnt: an all-pink outfit signals ditziness, white jeans convey country club privilege, an orange jumpsuit or dress is bold and unconventional, and all-black clothing and make-up indicate a propensity towards Gothic melancholy.

Fashion designers have also become entwined with certain colours: Coco Chanel's little black dress, the red of Valentino, the orange box of Hermès, the neutral browns and creams of Ralph Lauren and Max Mara, and the green of Prada. In wider popular culture, colours can trigger an association depending on how they're used in films, television series and music videos. There are the common tropes of the sexually confident woman in a red dress who we can't take our eyes off, or the villain who is often dressed in black (or white to subvert expectation), and the use of yellow to convey a moment of joy and happiness.

Over the centuries, colours have drifted in and out of fashion, creating new meanings as they filter through different strata of society. In ancient Rome, yellow was reserved for women, black for mourning, and Tyrian purple for emperors and royalty, because of the expense of extracting the precious dye from the gland of a species of sea snail. Christian artwork around 1000 BCE also set conventions around colour, with white as the symbol of purity, red as the blood of Christ, and blue for the Virgin Mary.

In the sixteenth century, under a wave of religious repression in Europe, black was the dominant colour of clothing because it represented piety, but by the 1950s, it had become a symbol of both sophistication and of rebellion. The ornately dressed courtiers and aristocrats of the French courts in the eighteenth century chose pale lemons, peach and cornflower for their doorway-busting *robes à la française*. In the Regency period, so associated with the works of Jane Austen, drawing rooms were filled with white gauzy muslin gowns, as neoclassical fashions followed a desire for simplicity and egalitarianism.

Our concepts around how we perceive colours, as well as their position next to one another, has shifted over many centuries. The ancient Egyptians assigned meaning to each of their six basic colours – black, white, red, green, blue and yellow – by which each one represented such powerful notions as life, death, fertility or victory. The ancient Greek writer Homer confusingly described the sky as bronze, the sea as wine-coloured, and sheep as violet. When his work was studied in the nineteenth century, the descriptions seemed so baffling, the assumption was

Goth singer
Siouxsie Sioux,
1980.

made that perhaps the Greeks were colour-blind. A couple
of centuries after Homer, the ancient Greek philosopher
Empedocles (444–443 BCE) considered four categories of
colour: white, black, red and yellow.

It wasn't until the seventeenth century that red,
yellow and blue were classified as primary colours, and
green, orange and purple as secondary ones. By carrying
out experiments with a glass prism, and a tiny hole in
a partition board, the English mathematician Sir Isaac
Newton observed the light broken into the colours of the
rainbow, reflected on the wall of his darkened room at
Cambridge University. His findings revealed that white
light is the combination of the full colour spectrum, and
that the colours bend at difficult angles as they pass
through a prism. Violet, with the shortest wavelength,
bends the most, and red, with the longest wavelength, the
least. Placed in the middle is green. When Newton initially
published his findings in 1672, he introduced orange as one
of the newest colours to the spectrum, removing white and
black and designating them non-colours. The inclusion of
white and black as colours has been debated by artists and

scientists ever since, but as tangible hues for the purposes of fashion, they have long been achieved by complicated systems of bleaching and dyeing.

Humans have been colouring textiles for over 6,000 years, with some of the oldest archaeological finds uncovered at the ancient Egyptian site of Thebes, which revealed an indigo-dyed garment from around 2500 BCE, as well as a red belt dyed with madder, in the grave of Tutankhamun. Traditionally, textile dyes came from either plant sources – such as madder root for red, indigo and woad for blue, and weld or fustic for yellow – or from animal sources. These included the murex sea snail, whose glands created a purple dye, and the insects kermes and cochineal, which created a brilliant red when crushed.

The earliest dye techniques involved steeping plants in water, and soaking fabrics in the solution to stain them. But as these were found to fade quickly, an understanding developed that another substance was needed to fix the colour to the fibres of the fabric. These substances, such as metallic compounds of alum, iron or copper, or tannin-rich barks, are known as mordants. The word is derived from the Latin word *mordere*, meaning "to bite" or "to fasten".

Yellow and brown dyes could be sourced from the tannins in a wide variety of plants, but to achieve strong, jewel-coloured reds, greens and blues, and deep blacks was a much more complicated process. Over time, dyers developed skills and knowledge in how alkaline and acids could work with dyestuff to yield different shades and tones. As the textile industry developed in the twelfth century in Europe, and bold, fast colours became beloved of the noble classes, guilds were formed to regulate all aspects of the business, to ensure there was a consistency in quality.

A series of sumptuary laws were introduced in the Middle Ages to limit certain colours of clothing to particular classes of people. In 1197, Richard the Lionheart stipulated that paupers could only wear the roughest, dullest cloth, and later, the Act of 1483 restricted the use of purple silk to members of the royal family. These laws created a hierarchy of dress and an instant visual statement, ensuring the poorest knew their place in society – with their dreary browns and washed-out blues and greens a sharp contrast to the wealthiest noblemen, in their vibrant red silks and shimmering golds.

For the Tudors, magnificent jewels, furs and brilliantly coloured textiles were powerful tools in conveying their domination, as there was a constant threat that they may be usurped by their rivals with claims to the throne. The meeting between Henry VIII and King Francis I of France became known as the Field of Cloth of Gold, for the resplendent luxury gold cloth and jewels that the two kings wore to demonstrate their power to one another.

A 1546 portrait of the teenage Princess Elizabeth depicts her wearing a fashionable crimson gown covered with pearls and jewels. Later, as Queen, she realized that wearing white and black made a more dramatic statement among the ladies of the English court, who were often dressed in red; this technique was also adopted by her cousin, Mary, Queen of Scots.

Certain colours were also used to stigmatize sections of society. Red was for prostitutes and executioners, yellow for forgers, heretics and Jews, and green for musicians and clowns. Traces of these colour conventions have remained in place, with the red lights of brothels common in cities around the world, and the painful history of the yellow star forced on Jews by the Nazis during the Second World War.

The discovery of the sea route to India by Vasco da Gama in 1498 allowed dyers to import large quantities of new dyes such as brazilwood, saffron, turmeric and indigo, thereby increasing the range of colours and improving the quality of dyed fabrics. But it was the eighteenth century that saw breakthroughs in the development of synthetic dyes that would revolutionize the industry. In 1737, the

French government began appointing a leading chemist as the inspector of dye works to support chemical research, and in 1789, that dye inspector, Claude Louis Berthollet, developed chlorine bleach. This invention was a huge improvement from bleaching fabric under the sun with the aid of lye and buttermilk.

In the nineteenth century, fuelled by the Industrial Revolution, new synthetic dyes were discovered by chemists including William Perkin, whose purple dye mauveine triggered a wave of novel, and sometimes toxic, dyes, including a version of madder, in 1869, and indigo, in 1878. That same year, a new group of synthetic dyes known as organic azo dyes, which are the basis of the dyes we use today, were invented.

The fashion industry took off in the twentieth century, as a whole range of synthetic dyes was developed to colour fabrics as cheaply as possible. As clothing became much more accessible, with the latest fashions outlined on the pages of *Vogue,* and later *Elle* and *Marie Claire*, consumers could easily discover the hottest colour trends – whether it was black, or whatever was being billed as "the new black". Purple, brown, and orange have all, at one time, been hailed as the next big thing.

This book sets out to explore the symbolism behind 10 colours – black, purple, blue, green, yellow, orange, brown, red, pink and white – and the significance they hold in costumes and clothing, from the ancient Egyptians to the Middle Ages, the Renaissance to the Victorian era, and popular culture over the last century. Colours, and their dyes, have fascinating but troubling histories; they have fuelled trade around the world, funded empires and reaped great wealth at the expense of others. Colours are proven to have been some of the most precious commodities in the world. These are their stories.

It's daybreak on a deserted Fifth Avenue and a taxi pulls up outside Tiffany's. A woman steps out, dressed in a long black evening gown and sunglasses, and a large pearl choker around her neck. As she pauses by the window of Tiffany's, she pulls out a coffee and a Danish pastry from a paper bag, and wistfully glances at the jewellery on display. It's that time of the morning before the city comes alive with rush-hour workers, and it's clear that the woman, Holly Golightly, dressed in elegant black, has been out all night. The film is, of course, *Breakfast at Tiffany's* (1961), and Audrey Hepburn's wardrobe of little black dresses, designed by Hubert de Givenchy, helped to define inky black as a code for sophistication and chic hedonism. When we think of black gowns, another decadent image may come to mind: Anita Ekberg in *La Dolce Vita* (1960), dancing in the Trevi Fountain after an evening in a Roman nightclub, her tight strapless gown precariously threatening to slip down.

Black

As one of the most powerful shades in fashion, black becomes a canvas that adapts to new interpretations and meanings. A black polo neck on a beatnik in a smoky dive bar in Greenwich Village in the 1950s was considered radically bohemian, but by the 1990s it was a wardrobe staple bought from the Gap and worn with high-waisted jeans; a look we now refer to as "normcore".

As well as being timelessly stylish, it can represent grief and loss when worn for mourning, or serve as a political tool, whether on the wrong or right side of history – as a symbol of fascistic threat in the uniform of Mussolini's Blackshirts or, with the berets of the Black Panthers, a powerful statement to push for civil rights. When founding the Black Panther Party in 1966, Bobby Seale and Huey Newton chose an urban-militant uniform of black beret, black leather jacket and shades for men and women alike, to create, as Seale described, "good visuals" to "capture the imagination of the people." The black beret was chosen for its revolutionary spirit as it was worn by Che Guevera and the French Resistance in the Second World War. Wearing black further reinforced the concept of the Black Panthers, in demonstrating strength and pride in being African American.

As well as being loaded with meaning, black can also symbolize the absence of expression – and as a result express even more. Godfather of punk Malcolm McLaren once said: "Black expressed the denunciation of the frill. Nihilism. Boredom. Emptiness." Similarly, Japanese designers in the 1980s like Issey Miyake, Yohji Yamamoto, and Rei Kawakubo of Comme des Garçons chose black as a response to the garish excesses of the decade. As Yamamoto told Suzy Menkes of the *New York Times* in September 2000: "Black is modest and arrogant at the same time. Black is lazy and easy – but mysterious. It means that many things go together, yet it takes different aspects in many fabrics. You need black to have a silhouette. Black can swallow light, or make things look sharp. But above all black says this: 'I don't bother you – don't bother me!'"

Black as a colour

Whether or not black is a colour has been hotly debated by scientists and artists for centuries. Black is what we see when an object swallows up all visible wavelengths, absorbing all light in the colour spectrum. Therefore, true black is the absence of colour.

On Isaac Newton's discovery of the spectrum in 1665, he deregulated both black and white when presenting a new order of colours. It wasn't until modernist artists of the twentieth century returned to black that it was given status as a colour. In 1946, Galerie Maeght on Paris's Left Bank staged the *Black is a Colour* exhibition, as a way of shocking the art establishment that had for so long championed Leonardo da Vinci's claim that black is not a colour. When capturing their landscapes, Impressionist painters had turned away from black. As Paul Gauguin said: "reject black and that mixture of black and white called gray." As a rare exception, Pierre-Auguste Renoir was influenced by black, often using it to shade the dark gowns of the Parisian women in his paintings.

While its status may be debated, black is undeniably one of the oldest pigments. In the Upper Palaeolithic era, black was created by using fire to burn wood, bark or shells to cinders. The ancient Egyptians also used carbon, along with manganese oxide from soil, for painting their hieroglyphics. Egyptians lined their eyes with kohl as it was believed to have magical properties that would protect against evil. While the poor would use soot, wealthier Egyptians could afford galena, a form of lead sulphide, which had properties that could prevent the risk of eye infections.

Lampblack, a black pigment of pure carbon from soot, was common during the prehistoric period and throughout the ancient world, where it was used to paint the walls of Egyptian tombs and for black-figure pottery in ancient Greece, but for dyeing textiles it proved more difficult. The results were often uneven or drab, and so black-dyed cloth was often relegated to the peasant classes up until the Middle Ages. When the Black Death swept across Europe starting in 1346, it wiped out one third of the population. With death so widespread, art of this period depicted the macabre – of skeletons and ghouls – as a response to so much suffering. Black was commonly worn in funeral processions by those casting last rites, but it also served as a symbol of morality. Wearing humble fabrics was thought to be an appeal to God for penance, as the plague was considered a punishment for wrongdoing. By the early Middle Ages, Christianity had developed strict moral codes whereby those who dressed excessively were considered sinful, while those who chose sober black clothes were righteous.

Yet black was also becoming popular among the merchant classes in Europe. Following the introduction of sumptuary laws in the Middle Ages, certain colours, like purple and red, and fabrics, like silk and gold cloth, were reserved for royalty and the aristocracy. Successful Italian merchants who had the wealth to afford the finest fabrics, but were restricted from wearing Venetian scarlet, turned to black. It was a modest colour without restrictions, and so they demanded the boldest, strongest blacks from buyers to achieve a sense of luxury in their clothing and display their burgeoning social status, while also remaining virtuous. High-quality black cloth became known as "sobelins" or "sabelins", after sable, a black fur which was much prized.

While scarlet silks were a proud feature of fifteenth-century Italian portraits, by the sixteenth century, black was the colour of choice for Renaissance sitters, as it was a marker of wealth and good taste. "Black is more pleasing in clothing than any other colour," said Italian courtier and author Baldassare Castiglione. As Paula Hohti Erichsen notes in her research on Renaissance fashion, post-mortem inventories from Venice, Florence and Sienna between 1550 and 1650 reveal that over 40 per cent of all artisans' clothes noted by colour were described as black.

As the wearing of black filtered upwards to the nobility and to royal courts across Europe, it became a symbol of prestige. King Philip II of Spain strongly favoured the black that reflected his defence of Catholicism against the Ottoman Empire. His reign saw Spain become the most powerful country in the world, and his taste for simple, unadorned, black drifted across Europe and into the Tudor courts of England.

Catherine of Aragon, Henry VIII's first wife, promoted her Spanish heritage by favouring dark velvets and silks for her Spanish farthingales, a hooped petticoat worn under skirts to expand the silhouette, and black gable headdresses to represent her piousness. After the excesses of her father's reign, Mary I dressed soberly in black and carried on this Spanish tradition following her marriage to Philip II of Spain in 1554, as she sought to reinstate Catholicism. In one portrait of the couple, by Lucas de Heere, Mary is seated on a throne wearing a black gown over a gold kirtle, or outer petticoat, as husband Philip stands beside her in black doublet and gold breeches. Their costume is both magnificent and devout, reflecting the religious symbolism of dressing in black.

From Puritanism to sorcery

The seventeenth century in Europe was a period marked by war, misery and religious conflict. From 1640 to 1649, England was under the dictatorial control of Oliver Cromwell, and his gloomy Puritanism affected all aspects of life. While black was still a fashionable colour, as demonstrated by a 1653 portrait of his wife,

Elizabeth Bourchier, wearing expensively dyed black velvet, it was also expected to be worn to show virtuosity and temperance. According to Lutheran reformer Philip Melanchthon in a sermon in 1537, colours that "clothe men like peacocks" should be eradicated, as flashy dress was a reminder of original sin.

The Puritan and Calvinist costume – of a dark gown for women and doublet and pantaloons with simple white collars and a tall black hat for men – was carried over to America by the pilgrims escaping persecution in Britain. New England's seventeenth-century Puritan colonies were particularly strict on dress codes, with sumptuary laws in place to ensure that clothing was appropriately modest. The Massachusetts Bay Colony introduced its first restrictions on dress in 1634, prohibiting new fashions, elaborate accessories or cloth woven with gold thread or lace, limiting the wardrobe of regular people to sober, dark and dull cloth.

As women were further repressed by the religious fundamentalism of the period, a fearful obsession with witchcraft grew in both Europe and colonial America. The belief in witches was easily spread by the printing revolution taking place in the fifteenth century – black letterings and engravings on white paper, depicting grotesque women's bodies raising storms and embracing the devil during a "sabbat", were disseminated widely. This ritual was thought to be held at night, in forests or ruins, where they stripped off their black clothing to take part in mass orgies that summoned the devil and his black creatures, like the bat, the crow and the black cat. To put it simply, black was the colour of evil.

Humans have always been afraid of the dark, particularly on the blackest of nights, without a moon in the sky, when everything is cloaked in shadow. It's a place of fear, where dangerous creatures lurk, and its impenetrable blackness acts as a cover for these sinister forces at work.

THE ULTIMATE JUSTICE OF THE PEOPLE·

1. Black Panther
Party members
demonstrating
at the New York
County Criminal
Court, April 1969.

2. *Portrait of
Madame X*
(1883–1884),
John Singer
Sargent.

1

2

In ancient mythology, the terror of darkness is also connected with the colour black. Nyx, the Greek goddess of the night, is clothed in black as she rides on a chariot pulled by four black horses. Nyx gives birth to what we consider the horrors of night – sleep, dreams, anguish, secrets, discord, distress, old age, misfortune and death – and her dark appearance is so frightening that she even scared the all-powerful Zeus. In illustrations in the Byzantine-era Paris Psalter manuscript, dating from around 950 CE, Nyx is depicted in a black robe, holding swathes of blue fabric.

When Shakespeare wrote *Macbeth* in 1606, he tapped into the hysteria around witchcraft and King James I's deep-seated fear of witches. In 1604, under James's rule, witchcraft was made a capital offence and thousands of women across the British Isles were put on trial, tortured and burnt alive. Shakespeare knew his audience would feel fear and fascination at the three "weird sisters", who owed a similarity to the three Fates of ancient mythology. They controlled the destiny of mankind with their spinning of white wool, but used black wool to weave a short life of misery.

Later, during the gothic revival of the eighteenth century, the witch swathed in black became a standard in paintings by artists like Francisco Goya. Daniel Gardner's *The Three Witches from Macbeth* (1775) was a portrait of Elizabeth Lamb, Viscountess Melbourne; Georgiana, Duchess of Devonshire; and Anne Seymour Damer, depicting them as good witches, throwing flowers into the cauldron instead of the toads and snakes of Shakespeare. Damer in particular wears what would become the stereotypical outfit of the witches – the black pointed hat and the long black dress.

The gloom across Europe lifted with the Age of Enlightenment from 1715, shifting fashion from Puritanical black to light and luminous tones – with women dressed in a range of sorbet hues, including lemon yellow, pale pink and powder blue. But a new trend for the macabre, and for black clothing, among those who considered themselves outsiders, was sparked by the publication of the first Gothic novel, *The Castle of Otranto* by the eccentric Horace Walpole, in 1764. Social anxieties around the terror of the French Revolution may also have contributed to an interest in dark romanticism in literature.

The Romantic poets – a group including Lord Byron, Percy Bysshe Shelley and John Keats – could be considered the goths or beatniks of the early nineteenth century. In portraits, they dressed in melancholic black, with their body often leaning and their head against their hands, as if tormented by their existential thoughts, and with a foresight that they would die young. In Caspar David Friedrich's *Wanderer Above the Sea of Fog* (1818), the black-clad figure is a lonely Romantic hero. He contemplates the sublime landscape with the demeanour of the beat poets who would follow his example 130 years later.

When Byron, Shelley, Mary Wollstonecraft Shelley and John Polidori took part in a ghost story contest near Lake Geneva in 1815, the result was Mary Shelley's *Frankenstein*, the first modern horror story, and Polidori's *The Vampyre*, based on Byron's story. The vampire character, Lord Ruthven, is an alluring, dangerous seducer, often depicted wearing a black coat like those of the Romantic poets, and would be the template for Bram Stoker's *Dracula* (1897). Stoker conjured up images of Byron in his description of a decadent Dracula, "clad in black from head to foot without a single speck of colour about him anywhere."

The Victorian cult of mourning
When Francis I, Holy Roman Emperor, died from a sudden stroke in 1765, the Holy Roman Empress Maria Theresa (the mother of Marie Antoinette) fell into complete mourning. The Habsburg ruler cut her long hair off, covered her apartments in black velvet, retreated from social events

and chose to wear nothing but black for the rest of her life, carving out a new identity as a mournful widow.

The custom of wearing black to commemorate the death of a loved one or ruler dates back to the ancient Greeks and Romans, who considered black the colour of death. But in Europe, black wasn't always the colour of mourning for royals. In the Middle Ages, widowed French queens glowed in white mourning clothing, or *deuil blanc*. When Anne of Brittany, first the wife of Charles VIII and then of Louis XII, chose to follow the Breton tradition of black for mourning rather than white, it caught on. The ruthless Catherine de' Medici famously wore black upon the death of her husband Henry II in 1559. The fashion spread out to other classes, who wished to emulate the elite in their outward display of grief. White remained a colour of mourning for royals in France up until the reign of Louis XVI and Marie Antoinette, but for those who were less wealthy, black was an accessible, cheaper and less high-maintenance colour to wear.

By the late 1830s, formal funereal black clothing was well established among the middle and upper classes, but the cult of mourning reached its peak in the reign of Queen Victoria, following the death of her husband Prince Albert in 1861. Intricate and ever-shifting rules were published in etiquette manuals. These affected the whole household, including the servants, but it was widows who were given the strictest social rules. Women were expected to remain in mourning for a couple of years after the death of their husbands, with progression through different stages to "half-mourning", where they could add white touches to their black gowns, or wear purple or grey. Many older women, like Queen Victoria, chose to reject all colour and wear only black for the rest of their lives.

With a nascent public interest in the style, mourning clothing became a fashion in itself, with one American etiquette book, *The Illustrated Manners Book* by Robert

DeValcourt, published in 1855, stating: "Black is becoming, and young widows, fair, plump, and smiling, with their roguish eyes sparkling under their black veils are very seducing." Many wealthy women chose sumptuous silks and velvets, and added aesthetic touches like plunging necklines, sequins and off-the-shoulder sleeves. As a striking widow in a fashionable gown inevitably attracted admirers, it was wryly noted that the trap was "re-baited".

After the death and destruction of the First World War, the concept of wearing black for mourning seemed too grim as nations dealt with collective grief. Instead, wearing black for evening wear became a byword for style and sophistication. The most memorable moment in the twentieth century for a grieving widow in black was at the funeral of John F. Kennedy in 1963, where Jackie Kennedy's anguished expression and tears were barely visible behind her heavy black veil. She was dressed simply in a black Givenchy suit, allowing her discreet mourning clothes to communicate her pain.

The femme fatale

While the dominant image of the woman in black was that of a widow, the colour was also fashionable for evening gowns during the Victorian era. John Singer Sargent's portrait of Madame Pierre Gautreau, dressed in a cleavage-revealing black satin dress with tiny, jewelled straps, caused such outrage when it was shown at the Paris Salon in 1884 that he later renamed it *Madame X* to protect her identity. Her confident pose, suggesting she is in complete control of her sexuality, marked her as a threat to women's traditional place in society. As we see through depictions of the femme fatale, the sensual power of the black dress inevitably leads to the downfall of the woman who chooses to wear it.

In *Anna Karenina*, Leo Tolstoy describes Anna attending a St Petersburg ball dressed in black. While the innocent Kitty is at first surprised by Anna's choice of gown, she realizes that for Anna, powerful in her beauty and confidence, black was the only colour for her to wear:

> Kitty had been seeing Anna every day; she adored her, and had pictured her invariably in lilac. But now seeing her in black, she felt that she had not fully seen her charm. She saw her now as someone quite new and surprising to her. Now she understood that Anna could not have been in lilac, and that her charm was just that she always stood out against her attire, that her dress could never be noticeable on her. And her black dress, with its sumptuous lace, was not noticeable on her; it was only the frame, and all that was seen was she – simple, natural, elegant, and at the same time gay and eager.

This moment at the ball, in a black dress as she dances with Count Vronsky, represents a time when Anna is at her happiest, commanding attention and adoration. But following her doomed affair with Vronsky, her divorce and the separation from her child, she is marked as an adulteress, and descends into sorrow and despair.

The association between black and the morally corrupt woman that Anna exemplifies was also evident on the silver screen. From the birth of the Hollywood film industry, black costumes were used to indicate that a character was bad. The vamp dressed in black became a character trope, following Theda Bara in *Sin* (1915) with her long, lank black hair and a black strapless dress. In the film noir genre that emerged at the end of the Second World War, the femme fatale in black satin was a fallen angel, reflecting the suspicions men felt when they returned home to find their wives and girlfriends now working and living independently. In *The Killers* (1946), Ava Gardner slinks panther-like onto the screen as Kitty Collins, in a black satin gown designed by Vera West. Such is her beauty and her power that men will cheat, steal and kill for her.

Also in 1946, Rita Hayworth starred in *Gilda*, where she performed one of her most famous musical numbers, a striptease to 'Put the Blame on Mame', in a column of strapless black satin, which was designed by Jean Louis and, in fact, inspired by *Madame X*. "There never was a woman like Gilda" was the strapline on posters, depicting Rita with her head tilted back provocatively, her red hair falling around her shoulders. The black dress was supposed to indicate that she was a morally repugnant woman who is cheating on her husband – yet she uses the bad-girl costume as an act to disguise her true, and good, intentions. "When I did the Gilda dress it was bolder and sexier than film designs of the time, but on Rita it was not vulgar," said Jean Louis.

In Hitchcock's *Psycho* (1960), Janet Leigh (as the character Marion Crane) switches from white to black underwear after she steals money from the bank where she works. In the nineteenth century, underwear was expected to be white, for purity, and it was considered sinful to wear black. Marion's black bra and slip not only mark her as deviant, but act as a signifier for her crimes, which ultimately lead her to the Bates Motel and to her horrific murder in the shower.

Black continues to be the colour of choice for the morally ambiguous femme in the movies, from Linda Fiorentino in *The Last Seduction* (1994) to Monica Bellucci in *Under Suspicion* (2000). Our first glimpse of the Italian star in the latter film is a voyeuristic shot of her pouring into a skin-tight, black Dolce & Gabbana gown, worn without underwear. As Mia Wallace in *Pulp Fiction* (1994), Uma Thurman wears a black jacket and cigarette pants, accessorized with a sleek black bob and Chanel Rouge Noir nails – her feminized version of the gangster suits worn by Samuel L Jackson and John Travolta.

The colour black to indicate an evil temptress was

played to great effect in *Black Swan* (2010). The costumes designed by Amy Westcott reflect Nina's transition from the pink and white ballet clothing that represents her emotionally stunted girlishness to the gradual inclusion of black and grey as her mind becomes more warped. The black feathers and tulle as worn by the black swan of *Swan Lake* is the final pinnacle in Nina's journey as she fully embraces her dark side.

The Little Black Dress

In 1926, Coco Chanel was credited with introducing the Little Black Dress to the world when her black crêpe de Chine sheath dress, worn with a gleaming string of pearls, was hailed by *Vogue* as the innovative equivalent of the Ford motor car. The fashion magazine predicted it becoming an everyday essential, and described it as "little" because it was discreet.

Coco Chanel's appreciation of simple black was inspired by her childhood spent in the convent at Aubazine Abbey. To her, black represented memories of austerity and of the nun's habits, the schoolgirl uniforms and the dark recesses of the abbey. Chanel also spoke of her inspiration for dressing women in black when she saw the bright jewel-coloured Paul Poiret gowns at a ball in Paris in 1920. She said that "black wipes out everything else around". While Chanel is often hailed as creator of the LBD, the first reference to the concept of the "Little Black Dress" is dated to 1902, in Henry James's *The Wings of the Dove*: "She might fairly have been dressed tonight in the little black frock ... that Milly had laid aside," he wrote. Despite Chanel's dismissive comments on his colourful gowns, Paul Poiret also took up black in the 1910s, and other designers followed suit.

After the outbreak of war in 1914, darker shades were more practical at a time when increasing numbers of women were working outside of the home. Writing to a friend in 1920, Marie Curie, famous for her pioneering research on radioactivity, said, "I have no dress except the one I wear every day. If you are going to be kind enough to give me one, please let it be practical and dark so that I can put it on afterwards to go to the laboratory."

In 1927, one of Hollywood's leading costume designers, Travis Banton, introduced the Little Black Dress to the silver screen when he dressed Clara Bow in the hit film *It*. Shopgirl Betty Lou struggles to find a dress to wear for a date at the Ritz, but her flatmate helps her to transform her simple black work dress into a daring cocktail dress. *It,* and Clara Bow's black dress, made an immediate impact on the working girls who flocked to the cinemas to see their favourite star on screen. By the end of the 1920s, filmmakers relied increasingly on black gowns to pop on monochrome film, making an immediate, bold impact.

By the 1950s, black had been adopted by every leading designer as the standard for elegance. Christian Dior launched his radical New Look in February 1947, with black dresses that were nipped in at the waist and used swathes of fabric to celebrate the end of wartime austerity. "You can wear black at any time," said Dior. "You can wear black at any age. You can wear it on almost any occasion. A little black frock is essential to a woman."

In 1952, Hubert de Givenchy was the 25-year-old boy wonder of fashion design who had just opened his own Parisian atelier. When a little-known actress called Audrey Hepburn came to his salon the following year, Givenchy agreed to help select some outfits, which were to fit the narrative for a Paris makeover in her next film, *Sabrina*. He created a design for a little black dress with a bateau neckline, and this was adapted for the screen by the film's costume designer Edith Head.

Givenchy's *Sabrina* dress set a trend, and solidified his close relationship with Hepburn, leading him to design

1. A beatnik outside the Gaslight Cafe, Greenwich Village, New York, 1959.

2. Marilyn Monroe at the Ambassador Hotel, New York, March 1955.

3. Members of the Vampyre Society at Whitby's Gothic weekend, 1992.

4. A model wearing Rick Owens at the CR Runway x LuisaViaRoma 90th anniversary, 2019.

a series of black dresses for her as the flighty courtesan Holly Golightly in *Breakfast at Tiffany's* (1961). The costumes were close to those in Truman Capote's original novella, where he described Holly as having one black dress for evenings and another for daytime, and envisioned his protagonist wearing "a slim cool black dress, black sandals, a pearl choker...A pair of dark glasses blotted out her eyes." While Holly Golightly is one of Hepburn's most beloved roles, it was in fact a part that Capote had insisted was only right for Marilyn Monroe.

Marilyn Monroe in black

At a news conference on 9 February 1956, 150 reporters and photographers scrambled into the Plaza Hotel as Marilyn Monroe made her first major appearance since escaping Hollywood – and her 20th Century Fox contract – in late November 1954. Her year in New York was a period of self-discovery; she formed her own production company and learnt method acting at the Actors Studio in New York. She also shook up her starlet wardrobe by opting for simple black slip dresses by Norman Norell, black wool coats and polo necks, all to suit the less showy Manhattan lifestyle that she was falling for. The clinging black slips and matte sheaths contrasted with her milky skin and luminous blonde hair, paring down her look for a cool, elegant appearance that balanced her fondness for wearing clothing a size too small.

At a photo shoot at the Ambassador Hotel, a relaxed Monroe was captured by photographer Eddie Feingersh in an intimate, déshabillé moment, giggling as she fitted herself into one of these Norell gowns in the bathroom. While Marilyn Monroe became forever known for her overtly sexual glamour, her Manhattan look was pioneering for the 1950s, with its raw, unvarnished style of dress.

The Plaza Hotel conference had been organized to announce that Monroe had taken control of her career and was set to star in and produce *The Prince and the Showgirl*, to be directed by the great and venerable Laurence Olivier. She made her entrance wearing a clinging black gown, but when one of the thin straps snapped, she was left to hold it up under the flash of jostling photographers, until she could find a safety pin to fix it. It was a wardrobe malfunction that generated headlines, but only served to horrify Olivier, who saw it as an attention-grabbing antic and immediately knew that their project was going to turn into a circus.

In late June 1962, *Vogue* arranged a photoshoot for the actress with photographer Bert Stern, in what would become known as The Last Sitting. Rather than pull the feature on the news of her death on 4 August 1962, *Vogue* published the images as a legacy to Monroe. The long-sleeved Dior dress, slashed at the back, acted to immortalize her as the authentic, glorious woman in simple black.

Black for rebellion

When Johnny Cash released his single 'The Man in Black' in 1971, the lyrics spoke of the reason that he chose to wear black instead of bright colours. He sang that it was for the poor and beaten down, the hopeless and hungry, the sick and old, and that he was in mourning for the "hundred fine young men" who were dying each week in the Vietnam War.

From his early days as a performer, Johnny Cash developed a stage uniform of black, which cemented his status as a rebel and an outsider. Black leather had become dangerously transgressive when worn by rockers and motorcyclists, as depicted by Marlon Brando in the 1953 film *The Wild One,* or on Elvis Presley. For Johnny Cash, his black leather showed his attitude and his grit.

During his now legendary Folsom Prison performance in 1968, Cash chose to wear a black three-piece suit and patent-leather loafers, with a slash of red lining in his jacket on display. His look bore a resemblance to that of the gunslinger in a western, but it also shared an ethos with the beat generation, a group of young, post-war idealists who rejected consumerism for a bohemian existence, expressing themselves through writing, jazz and Eastern philosophy.

They were represented by their de facto leaders, the writers Jack Kerouac and Allen Ginsberg, and to be a member, one had to show a degree of nonchalance, a sense of intellectual superiority and a lack of interest in the trappings of consumerism. In an essay in the *New York Times* in November 1952, Clellon Holmes described this post-war beat generation as feeling "a sort of nakedness of mind, and, ultimately, of soul; a feeling of being reduced to the bedrock of consciousness."

While the mainstream was dressing in excessive New Look fashions and preppy colours, the beat generation wore a simple silhouette that was nihilistically black. In New York's Greenwich Village, beat girls rejected the 1950s beauty-salon aesthetic in favour of black leotards and long straight hair, a look that coolly referenced Parisian existentialist Juliette Gréco. Known for her all-black outfits, Gréco described being a teenager in Paris after the war with only "one dress and one pair of shoes, so the boys in the house started dressing me in their old black coats and trousers. A fashion was shaped out of misery."

Such was the ubiquity of black polo necks, cigarette pants and sunglasses in subterranean coffee houses that beatniks became a parody of themselves, portrayed in films like *The Beat Generation* (1959) and *The Beatniks* (1960). When Audrey Hepburn visits a smoky Parisian beatnik bar in *Funny Face* (1957), she performs a dance dressed in black, with her costume and movements poking fun at both the existentialists of Paris's Left Bank and the beatniks of Greenwich Village.

Gothic youth culture

Inspired by the haunting photos of nineteenth-century widows swathed in black, the goth subculture, first emerging in the late 1970s, fully embraced the macabre with jet-black clothing that matched their eyeliner. The dark and morbid naturally appealed to youth cultures, and goth fashion was both rebellious and nostalgic – obsessed with a theatrical, amplified version of the past. It spoke the language of nineteenth-century Gothic literature, vampire fiction and medieval and Victorian rituals, creating a form of beauty from death and incorporating the symbolism of black from religious rites and mourning.

The original goth girl was Siouxsie Sioux, later the leader of the band the Banshees and a regular at Vivienne Westwood and Malcolm McLaren's punk shop SEX on the King's Road. It sold a range of black fetishwear and tapped into a new punk-rock response to the psychedelia of the hippie movement. The black dress was adapted into leather, or ripped and pinned, and worn by New Wave figureheads like Debbie Harry. Siouxsie Sioux and her followers went further by backcombing their hair, painting their faces white and outlining their eyes in inky black, and squeezing into black fishnets, leather miniskirts and black knee-high boots.

In 1982, The Batcave club opened in London, and with its motto "Blasphemy, Lechery, and Blood", it soon attracted a crowd of goth worshippers dressed in melodramatic black. Goth style was pastiche, in which Victorian corsets and mourning veils were combined with black PVC, leather with lace, and hair was mussed up as if from a night spent crawling out of a grave.

The youthful self-expression of Victorian costumes and theatrical make-up remained relatively outside of the mainstream (save for Robert Smith of The Cure), until Cher embraced goth style with her Bob Mackie spiderweb dress at the 1986 Academy Awards. In his Gothic fairytales, film director Tim Burton created melancholy icons out of Johnny Depp in *Edward Scissorhands* (1990) and Winona Ryder in *Beetlejuice* (1988). Both were classed as outsiders in their black costumes in a colourful world, their characters showing a greater vulnerability and deeper understanding of humanity than others.

Goth culture experienced a significant revival in the late 1990s, in part because of the ways those with similar interests could connect and share images over the internet. But the surge in headlines around their macabre antics also led to a moral panic in the United States. Goth teenagers were labelled as evil by Christian fundamentalists for the propensity to dress in black and for their interest in witchcraft and the occult.

The moral panic didn't take into account new branches of goth – the industrial goths with their black military style and shaved heads, or the cyber goths who mixed black with Day-Glo rave style. In Japan, a black Gothic twist on the Lolita subculture emerged in the late 1990s. While Lolitas dressed in cute pink and white Alice in Wonderland–style costumes, the Gothic version featured black crosses and dark make-up, and was first popularized by Japanese visual kei bands like L'Arc-en-Ciel and Malice Mizer. Gothic Lolita style allowed for young people to express their personalities and their love of the lifestyle through their clothing, which they could purchase through brands like Moi-même-Moitié, founded by visual kei musician Mana in 1999, and alice auaa, founded in 1995.

In the late 1990s, the actress Angelina Jolie established herself as a rebel with her tattoos, knife collection and habit of wearing a vial of her husband's blood around her neck. By the time she replicated a Morticia Adams' look at the 2000 Academy Awards by wearing a black Versace gown, with her dark hair long and loose, the goth subculture had been embraced by fashion designers like Alexander McQueen. (The erotic macabre has long held interest for designers. In 1938, Elsa Schiaparelli teamed up with Salvador Dalí for the skeleton dress, a black rayon dinner dress with the bones outlined in padded embroidery, shown in 1938 as part of her Circus collection.)

Black was the overarching colour for McQueen, who infused his designs with a sense of bleak romance and of persecution, such as his references to the Salem witch trials in his Autumn/Winter 2007 show. For his Autumn/Winter 2002/2003 collection, entitled "supercalifragilisticexpialidocious", he reimagined the Gothic fairytale with his mystical black creations, including a billowing black parachute cape.

Fashion designer Rick Owens was inspired by his teenage years as a goth in California when sketching his ideas. "When I see young goths on the street, I feel like they're my children," he said. Goth culture also reminded him of Catholic school, with "people in dragging robes, hooded figures doing spiritual things – everything I do comes from that". Owens gave birth to the notion of street goth, with his brutalist collections that fused sportswear with Gothic aesthetics. Its influence led to health goth, which first emerged from Tumblr, and by 2014 was one the most Googled subcultures; it combines a love of heavy metal and goth symbols like the pentagram with black sportswear and bio-tech elements. The #healthgoth hashtag on Instagram evolved into a wider culture that inspired brands like Adidas and Nike to turn their sportswear black.

When all else fails, the lesson is to wear black. Princess Diana wore an off-the-shoulder black dress by Christina Stambolian in June 1994, the same night that Prince Charles's tell-all documentary on their marriage was due to air. Labelled her "Revenge" dress, it highlighted how a black dress is the perfect blank canvas to define your identity. As Zandra Rhodes said in 2008, "A black dress is the best statement piece there is."

Following the news in April 2016 that the pop star Prince had died suddenly, shocked fans gathered in downtown Los Angeles to dance and sing to his music and to celebrate his life by wearing his signature colour. The *Los Angeles Times* interviewed Gilbert Aragon, 51, who was dressed in a purple fur vest and leather gloves. "It's the greatest thing you could do for him," said Aragon, who'd been a fan since he was 18 years old.

The singer-songwriter may have sung about other colours like 'Raspberry Beret' and 'Little Red Corvette', but it's 'Purple Rain' that he's forever connected with. Bathed in lilac smoke, dressed in a purple suit, and playing a custom-made purple guitar and piano, he wore purple throughout his career because he felt it gave him stage presence.

Purple

When his sister Tyka Nelson claimed in a 2017 interview that orange was really the musician's favourite colour, Prince's half-sister Sharon Nelson came out to defend purple. She said that while he "was fond of many colors in the rainbow, he especially loved the color purple because it represented royalty" and "the color purple always made him feel Princely".

From the ancient period, purple was the preserve of the most powerful. Named "imperial" or "royal" purple, it symbolized wealth and power, and could only be worn by emperors, royals and heads of churches. In Rome, Emperor Nero was so protective over his purple robes that any citizen caught wearing the colour would face exile, or even death. Its preciousness was due to its rarity. The dye originated in the ancient civilization of Phoenicia and was sourced from a small gland in murex snails, and to create the lustrous, rich dye was an incredibly time-consuming, complex and highly secretive process.

It wasn't until the chemist William Henry Perkin invented an artificial purple in 1856, which he named "mauveine", that fashionable silks could affordably be tinted a dazzling array of purples. As well as mauve and violet, there was lilac, plum, fuchsia, aubergine, wine, lavender, magenta, periwinkle, amaranth and heliotrope, all taking their names from flowers, fruit and vegetables.

As Alice Walker writes in the preface to her novel *The Color Purple* (1982), purple "is always a surprise but is found everywhere in nature". Purple is associated with the character of Celie, first as her favourite colour, and then as symbolic of the strength she needs to break away from her abusive husband, because purple indicates God's influence on Earth. Shug Avery tells Celie, "I think it pisses God off if you walk by the color purple in a field somewhere and don't notice it."

Shades of purple are perceptible in the natural world – in the petals on flowers, from the juices of succulent blueberries and blackberries, and on the glossy skin of aubergines. In the visible spectrum, "violet" has the shortest wavelength, making it the last one we see. Because of this, it's considered to be of a higher realm, offering a sense of spiritual awareness, which is perhaps why purple infused the art nouveau movement, the Pre-Raphaelites and the hippie subculture, which all embraced alternative thought and dress.

Purple is a colour that some people love, and others hate. Mauve in particular has old-fashioned connotations – couturier Neil "Bunny" Roger referred to a particular shade of muted purple as "menopausal mauve", given its associations with Victorian widows.

During the O.J. Simpson criminal murder trial, defence lawyer Johnnie Cochran wore a double-breasted suit in a shade that was much contested – was it periwinkle or grey-blue? "Just don't call it mauve," he said. This story was in contrast to his autobiography, *A Lawyer's Life,* where he reflected, "I do take great pride in the way I dress." He recalled a time when he was working as a lawyer in New York, and was asked by a reporter, "What's with the mauve suit?" Cochran described his cool response: "It's a mauve kind of day."

A purple fit for royalty

When the royal barge of Cleopatra (69–30 BCE) sailed into harbour, the first thing those on the shoreline noticed was the purple sails, dyed with the expensive secretions of sea snails, and perfumed to mask the pungent smell. The Egyptian queen was well aware that the colour purple further enhanced her glorious image, and as well as the purple drapes in her palace, the sails of her barge made an immediate impact, heralding her arrival. It was a moment captured by William Shakespeare in *Antony and Cleopatra* (1607): "The barge she sat in, like a burnish'd throne / Burned on the water: the poop was beaten gold / Purple the sails, and so perfumed that / The winds were lovesick with them."

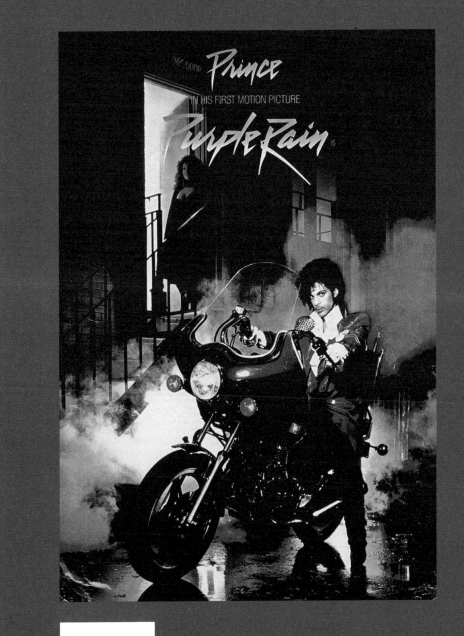

Poster for
Prince's *Purple
Rain*, 1984.

The most significant dye source for purple throughout the ancient world was a dye extracted from molluscs, and reserved exclusively for royalty. From around 1500 BCE, the heart of the purple dye trade was the ancient Phoenician city of Tyre, where Lebanon is now located. As they traded their purple textiles across the Mediterranean, Phoenician dye factories dotted the coastline from the Marmara Sea to Asia Minor, and around Greece. Factory sites, evident from the remnants of piles of shells, have also been found in Spain and West Africa.

Tyrian purple was harvested from several species of murex sea snail, which produced different shades of purple, varying from blue to red. One Phoenician legend outlined the origins of the precious dye. The god Melqart, patron of Tyre, was walking on the beach with his mistress when his pet dog fished a sea snail out of the water and began chewing on it. When Melqart noticed that his dog's mouth turned purple, this inspired him to use the snails to dye a gown of the same colour for his mistress, and to bless Tyre with the secrets of the dye, so as to bring it great wealth.

Fishing for these sea snails could only take place in autumn and winter, when the colour was at its strongest, and the creatures were kept alive until the secretion from the gland was extracted, otherwise it would be lost. This liquid appeared clear, but when it came into contact with oxygen, it turned a deep, long-lasting shade of purple. The liquid and the crushed shellfish were salted and fermented in wood ash and urine for three days, then left to simmer in a metal vat for 10 days.

Up to 12,000 sea snails were needed to create one gram of Tyrian purple, and it was a messy, smelly business, as vast amounts of flesh from the murex were discarded and left in the sun. The dye factories of Tyre were located outside the city walls, to protect the residents from the stench of rotting fish and urine.

Despite the smell, which Pliny described as "offensive", Tyrian purple was traded by the Phoenicians throughout the ancient world, and by the fourth century BCE it was worth decidedly more than gold. In ancient Rome, certain elite citizens wore a broad purple band on the edges of their white togas, including magistrates and freeborn children, while victorious generals were honored with the *toga picta*, an impressive Tyrian-purple cloth threaded with gold.

As the Romans expanded their empire and dominated the Mediterranean ports, the dye became even more significant. When Julius Caesar visited Egypt in 48 BCE, he was said to have been so impressed by the powerful image created by Cleopatra, with her exclusive use of the royal purple for her barge and as decoration in her palace, that he chose purple as symbolic of his power and introduced a rule for Imperial Rome allowing a triumphant general to wear an-all purple toga too.

By 300 CE, following the fall of the Roman Empire, production of Tyrian purple was transferred to Constantinople, the Byzantine capital, where purple maintained its status as a royal colour. The colour was so symbolic of royalty that empresses gave birth in chambers swathed in Tyrian purple cloth, so that it would be the first thing royal babies would see.

When Constantinople was seized by the Turks in 1453, the Byzantine Empire collapsed, and with it went the ancient skill of creating Tyrian purple. There is evidence of molluscs being used for purple dye in ancient Peru and by the Aztecs in Mexico, and archaeologists believe that small shellfish found on the coast of Cornwall and in Ireland were used to dye the clothes of church dignitaries. But after the secrets of Tyrian purple had been lost, new plant-based methods became the dominant means of creating the colour.

Despite the abundance of purple in nature, it's not easily achievable using plant sources. The simplest way to create purples was to dye fabric red with madder or brazilwood and then dip it in a vat of blue woad or indigo. In Japan, from around 800 CE, a deep purple called *murasaki*, named from the root from which it's extracted, was used for dyeing purple kimonos, which, again, were reserved only for royals.

While bilberry or whortleberry could create a purple dye alone, the most common, and important, flora was logwood, from a tree grown in parts of South America and the West Indies. When combined with different mordants, logwood could create strong colours ranging from black to purple. Dye could also be extracted from a lichen known as orchil, which was perilously collected from steep rock faces in southern Europe. While the ancient Greeks and Romans utilized it, this method was rediscovered in the fourteenth century by the Florentines, who created a monopoly in blues and purples derived from lichen, which they steeped in urine to prepare. Because these purple dyes didn't have the same lustrous qualities of Tyrian purple, the hue lost its exclusivity by the Renaissance period, and instead, red (obtained from kermes and cochineal) became the royal colour, indicating luxury and status. But purple still held a deep-seated significance. Despite there being no artistic depictions of him wearing the colour, Henry VIII introduced a sumptuary law in 1510 which stipulated that purple could only be worn by the king, or with his consent.

When Mary I was crowned queen, she wore a purple velvet gown to reinforce her significance as the first queen regnant in English history. Her sister, Elizabeth I, was similarly enamoured with purple; she wore a purple gown to her coronation banquet in 1559, and when she died in 1603, she stipulated that her coffin be draped in purple velvet.

Once the sumptuary laws were abandoned throughout Europe in the seventeenth century, purple could be worn by all classes. In the Enlightenment period of the eighteenth century, rich purples were considered too heavy and dark at a time when the fashion was for light, bright colours. It wasn't until the Victorian age, as elaborate gowns became a canvas for ever more inventive synthetic colours, that purple really thrived.

From mauveine to violetine

In 1856, when a young chemistry student named William Henry Perkin was carrying out a series of experiments in his home laboratory on the top floor of his parents' East End home, little did he know that his teenage research would lead to a revolution in the fashion industry, and a century later earn him his own blue plaque. Perkin had enrolled at the Royal College of Chemistry at the age of 15, and such was his promise that he had been working as an assistant to his professor, the celebrated German chemist August Wilhelm von Hofmann.

The gas that lit up cities across Britain, powering factories and houses, also left vast quantities of dangerous sulphur during its production, and scientists were competing to find a means for using up this residue. In Glasgow in the 1820s, Charles Macintosh developed a method of waterproofing cloth using coal tar, leading to the launch of raincoats that would bear his name. Hofmann saw the potential in tweaking the molecules of tar to synthesize quinine, the only known substance that could tackle the blight of malaria in Europe and Asia.

By the time he was 18, Perkin was carrying out his own home experiments to create quinine. After adding hydrogen and oxygen to coal tar in his glass beakers, he was left with a disheartening black sludge. As he began cleaning the jars with denatured alcohol, there was something intriguing enough for him to dip a piece of cloth into. When it came out "a strangely beautiful colour", as he described it, he realized he had created his own Tyrian purple. "On experimenting with the colouring matter thus obtained," he later wrote, "I found it to be a very stable compound dyeing silk a beautiful purple that resisted the light for a long time."

He patented his discovery in August 1856, and made the difficult decision to give up his studies in favour of commercially manufacturing his synthetic dye. With support from his family, Perkin built his factory in the north-west of London in 1857. But he experienced a setback when he failed to secure his patent in France, and discovered that factories were already producing a dye very similar to his in colour. Paris fashion periodicals were celebrating a new colour called "mauve", taken from the pink–purple of the mallow flower. The fashionable Empress Eugénie, wife of Emperor Napoleon III, decided that mauve matched her eyes. Inspired by Eugénie, Queen Victoria wore a mauve velvet gown to her eldest daughter Victoria's wedding to the Prussian Prince Frederick William in 1858.

Riding on the back of its popularity in French haute couture, Perkin combined "mauve" with "aniline" to name his dye "mauveine". He soon became an incredibly wealthy man, as its mass manufacture led to a prolific demand for his colour in women's fashion.

Charles Dickens wrote in 1859 in his literary magazine *All Year Round*, "As I look out of my window, the apotheosis of Perkin's purple seems at hand – purple hands wave from open carriages – purple hands shake each other at street doors – purple hands threaten each other from opposite sides of the street; purple-striped gowns cram barouches, jam up cabs, throng steamers, fill railway stations: all flying countryward, like so many birds of purple paradise."

In August of that same year, the satirical magazine Punch published a sketch entitled The Mauve Measles, linking the fever for mauve with an outbreak of measles in children in 1859, which caused purple-red spots across the skin: "The eruption, which is of a mauve colour, soon spreads, until in some cases the sufferer becomes completely covered with it."

Perkin's discovery of mauveine inspired a wild range of new synthetic dyes, and their popularity was further enhanced by the crinoline, the iron-birdcage structure worn underneath skirts to create a voluminous shape. Requiring yards and yards of fabric, crinolines became the perfect canvas for showcasing the fashionable new colours of the moment, with women transformed by designers like Charles Worth into brilliant "birds of purple paradise", as described by Dickens.

François-Emmanuel Verguin created a vivid red-purple by mixing aniline and tin chloride, which he called "fuchsine" from the flowering shrub fuchsia, and which became known in Britain as "Solferino" and "magenta" in 1859, after the locations of battles in the Second Italian War of Independence.

The rage for aniline had a detrimental effect on the natural dye industries, with demand for indigo and madder shrinking over the decades since Perkin's discovery. Worse, it was later discovered that a number of these miraculous new colours contained dangerous levels of arsenic, particularly fuchsine. When Perkin attempted his own magenta using mercuric nitrate, his workmen began to fall ill from mercury poisoning, and he put a halt to production. There were also stories of how the waters of the Grand Junction Canal by Perkin's factory were a different colour every week. In the 1860s, a dye factory in Basel, Switzerland, which produced fuchsine and aniline violet, was fined and forced to close after it was found guilty of pumping toxins into the water supply and poisoning the locals with arsenic.

By the early 1870s, mauve had waned in popularity among the younger generation, and was now most associated with mourning clothes, following Princess Alexandra appearing in a delicate mauve half-mourning gown in 1863. A reader of *The Englishwoman's Domestic Magazine* wrote to the resident fashion expert to ask what she should do with an old-fashioned bright mauve gown given to her by an aged relative. The magazine responded by agreeing "bright mauve is certainly old-fashioned, but is allowable as a house dress" and that "plentiful trimmings of dark military braid would tone the brilliancy a great deal".

In the United States, the 1890s, or the "Gay Nineties", were described by writer Thomas Beer in 1926 as "the mauve decade" because of the riches and excesses, but one writer who connected purple with a certain type of older woman was Oscar Wilde. In *The Portrait of Dorian Gray* (1890), he associated mauve with older women who were trying too hard to look young: "Ordinary women always console themselves. Some of them do it by going in for sentimental colours. Never trust a woman who wears mauve, whatever her age may be, or a woman over thirty-five who is fond of pink ribbons. It always means that they have a history." For his 1895 play *An Ideal Husband*, the attention-grabbing femme fatale Mrs Cheveley wore a dress in a bright purple described as "heliotrope".

Perhaps this was why purple developed an old-fashioned edge in Britain in the late Victorian era – it was being worn by too many older widows, who had adapted their purple dresses from the 1860s to use as mourning clothes. In the television series *Downton Abbey*, the old Dowager, Violet Crawley, played by Maggie Smith, was often costumed in Queen Alexandra–style gowns in mauve. This not only indicated in the first series that she was in mourning for her relatives who died on the *Titanic*, but was also a reference to it being a colour for older women. The colour still retained its royal mourning credentials into the 1950s. It was reported that when King George VI died in 1952, even mauve underwear was displayed in West End shop windows.

From art nouveau to art deco
After suffering a short illness, William Perkin died in 1907, 50 years after making his groundbreaking discovery of mauveine. By this time, he had been recognized and

celebrated for paving the way for advances in medicine, explosives and photography, creating the stepping stone to discovering the artificial sweetener saccharin, and his pioneering work in immunology and chemotherapy.

While purple had fallen out of fashion by the late nineteenth century, in the Edwardian era paler violets, lavenders and lilacs were back in vogue. When the Impressionists were painting "en plein air", they saw violet shades in the shadows and in the clouds, complimenting the yellow of sunlight. The light shades of purple suited the Edwardian need to embrace fresh, pale colours that counteracted the industrialization that blackened cities with soot. Following the aesthetics of the art nouveau and Arts and Crafts movements, purple tones appeared in swirling patterns on Aubrey Beardsley posters and on William Morris wallpaper, and in the velvet gowns and jackets worn with high-neck, delicate, pale lace blouses, as sold at Liberty & Co.

While purple was still being worn for mourning, it was adopted by the British suffragettes as one of the three colours to unify their movement in 1908. As Emmeline Pethick-Lawrence, the editor of the suffragette newspaper *Votes for Women*, wrote, purple was chosen for its long connection with royalty, for "the royal blood that flows in the veins of every suffragette, the instinct of freedom and dignity", along with white for purity and green as "the emblem of spring". In the United States, the National Woman's Party combined purple with white and gold, because, as outlined in a December 1913 newsletter, it was "the color of loyalty, constancy to purpose, unswerving steadfastness to a cause".

Thomas Beer's reflective study of the 1890s, *The Mauve Decade*, struck a chord with Jazz Age readers when it was published in 1926, as both decades had a sense of cultural experimentation and optimism. The 1920s reignited a fascination with brilliant hues, and mauve was described as "a favourite colour" in Paris in an April 1926 edition of *The Times*. In June 1925, it hailed "two shades of orchid mauve chiffon" as a cool fabric to wear for Ascot and Henley. A purple bias-cut satin evening gown by Jeanne Lanvin was the epitome of art deco elegance. Using one strong colour, the gown was shimmering and fluid, contrasting with its severe geometric collar.

The lavender decade

A *Life* magazine article in August 1961 revealed that "Kim Novak is passionate for purple. She writes purple prose on purple paper with lavender ink, wears purple clothing, sleeps between purple sheets and when her studio assigned her to throw a left-hand punch for her next film, *The Notorious Landlady*, she went out and bought a pale purple punch bag to practice on."

Novak, the star of the films *Picnic* (1955) and *Pal Joey* (1957), was regularly linked with the colour lavender as she emerged as one of the most popular stars of the 1950s. Not only was she described as having lavender-coloured eyes, but a 1956 feature in *Photoplay* entitled "The Girl with the Lavender Life" equated her favourite colour with the rosy outlook of her career. The article continued: "In Miss Novak's life lavender has become an all-important morale-builder, lavender being her word to describe rather inclusively all shades ranging from rich purple to pale lilac."

Just as the 1890s was considered "the mauve decade" for its optimism, the 1950s was a lavender decade, and shades of purple came back into fashion along with a rainbow of colours which represented optimism and consumerism. Lavender was a feminine colour that offered a soft alternative to popular pink, and was reminiscent of James Whistler's description of mauve as "just pink trying to be purple." The *New York Times*, on 12 June 1951, hailed lilac and mauve as "the most flattering tints" for maternity wear. In 1963, the newspaper credited the trend for purple, along

1. Kim Novak in *Jeanne Eagels* (1957).

2. Artwork by Margaret Morris for the song sheet of the suffragette anthem 'The March of the Women', 1911.

3. Pierre Balmain's A/W collection, 1958.

with other bright colours, to the influence of California on fashion: "At Christian Dior in Paris this afternoon, a gaunt model will sweep through a curtained doorway dressed in an ankle-length column of crepe. It is eggplant purple belted in neon pink and its name is 'Beverly Hills.'"

Elizabeth Taylor was exalted for her violet eyes, and she often wore purple to bring out the colour. In her starring role in the colossal film *Cleopatra* in 1963, her eyes were heavily made up with kohl and deep purple eyeshadow, for a 1960s twist on ancient Egypt. She had also worn deep purple gowns in her starlet publicity portraits in the 1950s, and at the 1970 Academy Awards she turned up the glam factor in a periwinkle-hued gown designed by Edith Head, which perfectly accentuated her hourglass figure and her St Tropez tan. During the 1980s and 1990s, a period marked by her AIDS activism and her lucrative perfumes, she continued to value the power of purple, wearing a series of purple satin cleavage-enhancing gowns with big sleeves, including for the 1988 launch of her scent Passion.

At the same time as it was being heralded for fashion in the 1950s, "lavender" was also a term that was used to denigrate the gay community in the United States. Referred to as "The Lavender Scare" by historian David K. Johnson, after the use of the derogatory term "lavender lads" for gay men, it was a period when 5,000 federal agency employees lost their jobs because of their sexuality. A decade later, lavender was reclaimed by the LGBTQ community following the Stonewall Riots of 1969, when lavender sashes and armbands were given to the crowds who were marching from Washington Square Park to The Stonewall Inn in New York, where riots had taken place a month before. As film director Derek Jarman wrote in his 1993 essay "Purple Passage": "Purple is passionate, maybe violet becomes a little bolder and FUCKS pink into purple. Sweet lavender blushes and watches", and that "purple is also an expression of being gay. The blue of men and the red of women combine to make queer purple."

In 1969, feminist activist Betty Friedan referred to the lesbian membership of the National Organization of Women as "the Lavender Menace". It led to a group of radical activists making the decision to wear purple T-shirts emblazoned with that expression at the Second Congress to Unite Women. Karla Jay, one of the organizers, recalled:

> ... both aisles were lined with seventeen lesbians wearing their Lavender Menace T-shirts and holding the placards we had made. Some invited the audience to join them. I stood up and yelled, "Yes, yes, sisters! I'm tired of being in the closet because of the women's movement." Much to the horror of the audience, I unbuttoned the long-sleeved red blouse I was wearing and ripped it off. Underneath, I was wearing a Lavender Menace T-shirt. There were hoots of laughter as I joined the others in the aisles ... Rita [Mae Brown] pulled off her Lavender Menace T-shirt. Again, there were gasps, but underneath she had on another one. More laughter. The audience was on our side.

Psychedelic purple

When Barbara Hulanicki opened her little boutique, Biba, in London in 1964, she immediately drew in a crowd of enthusiastic young women for her bohemian mod designs that harked back to the art nouveau movement at the turn of the century and the art deco of the 1920s. Through her fashion line, the designer, still in her twenties, sold romantic clothing in earthy tones like olive, rust and her favourite, "bruised purple". Rich purple velvet gowns and floppy mauve hats became a signature, as girls on a shop assistant's wages could buy into the affordable "total look" that Biba championed.

1. Model Twiggy in a promotion for Biba make-up, 1972.

2. Lavender Menace T-shirts worn by members of the lesbian radical feminist movement, 1970.

3. The Biba store, Kensington, 1972.

Hulanicki described her Biba girl as:

... dreamy and untouchable ... She was so young and fresh that all those Auntie colours that I had hated when I was young looked new on her. In the daylight the orchids, dusty blues, bilberries and mulberries looked quite in tune with her surroundings. Once she was inside Biba, the music thundered, the lighting was soft and she became more mysterious.

Biba became the meeting place for hip young people on Saturdays, and she described the impact of her shop as a cultural hub: "Years later I had letters from people who met at Biba, spent their courtship in Biba on Saturdays, married, had babies and wrapped them in Biba purple nappies."

As well as a reference to the art nouveau movement that had celebrated nature's colours, purple defined the sweeping psychedelia of the hippie movement of the late 1960s. The writer Tom Wolfe dubbed the 1960s "the purple decade" and compiled his journalism on the countercultural movements into a book of the same title.

Purple was a colour that seemed to represent the Summer of Love of 1967. In the Haight-Ashbury neighbourhood of San Francisco, purple was visible in the tie-dye shirts and flowers nestled in long hair, representing a new movement that celebrated the natural world and Eastern philosophy. Posters for rock bands and concerts, heavily indebted to art nouveau artists Alphonse Mucha and Aubrey Beardsley, used a trippy combination of tangerine and aubergine, or fuchsia and emerald – colour combinations that were off-centre. It translated into fashion, with a 1966 article in the *New York Times* entitled "Orange on Purple: Colors on the Young", describing "Orange circles on a purple suit ... Color as savage as the rhythmic blasts from a transistor radio."

Jimi Hendrix linked purple to smoky psychedelia with the song 'Purple Haze' describing being so high on drugs that all he could see was purple. While it was a reference to the "purple Monterey" variety of LSD, as well as to the purple, heart-shaped uppers prevalent throughout the 1960s, it was also symbolic of the confusion of purple, where blue and red blend to become so many different shades and tones.

Prince and purple

Often nicknamed The Purple One, the artist and musician Prince was entwined with the colour, which seemed to suggest decadence and excess. So much so that in August 2017, the Prince estate worked with Pantone to develop his own purple, Love Symbol No.2.

Prince first began wearing purple during the period of his fourth album, *Controversy*, in 1982, when he wore a mauve custom-dyed trench coat. While performing on The 1999 Tour, he jotted down on a purple notebook his concept for his movie and album *Purple Rain*. When released in 1984, they would become a phenomenal success, firming up his reputation as a visionary, and forever linking him to the purple of his embellished satin jackets, the smoke that washed over him on stage, and his New Romantic, gender-defying style.

Casci Ritchie, Prince expert and author of *On His Royal Badness: The Life and Legacy of Prince's Fashion* (2021), says: "The most obvious thing about him liking purple is that it relates to royalty ... It played into the mystique and intrigue of his persona and helped to reinforce a self-created myth around him. Purple is quite a unique colour, and it allowed him to have a colour that was specifically his."

Prince provided the soundtrack to the 1989 movie *Batman*, where his music punctuated scenes with the Joker (Jack Nicholson). From his inception in the first comic book in 1940 to Heath Ledger's acclaimed performance in *The Dark Knight* (2008), the character is

1. Beyoncé performing 'Crazy in Love' at the BET Awards, 2003.

2. Givenchy, A/W 2018/2019.

regularly depicted in an off-beat purple coat that clashes with garish oranges or greens, a style that demonstrates his madness and ambition. In one scene in the 1989 film, Kim Basinger's Vicky Vale acts as if she is trying to seduce the Joker, telling him, "you're so powerful. And purple. I love purple." Perhaps this particular moment was an inside joke, as Basinger and Prince were dating at the time, having met during production.

Purple has further infused pop music through the wardrobe of one of the genre's greatest stars: Beyoncé. During her period in Destiny's Child, the group members dressed in coordinated shimmering lilac and magenta minidresses and jumpsuits designed by her mother Tina Knowles. For her high-octane performance on stage for the BET Awards in 2003, going solo with her breakthrough single 'Crazy in Love', Beyoncé chose a plunging purple gown with lime-green detail from Versace's Spring/Summer 2003 collection, which she slashed to the thigh. It made an immediate impact as the moment that marked her as a global superstar and queen of pop. Eighteen years later, Zendaya wore the original floor-length version of the sheer Versace gown for the BET awards in 2021, which had been sourced by her stylist, and not only paid tribute to Beyoncé's iconic performance, but captured the nostalgia for fashions from the turn of the millennium.

Purple power

"Forget about the avocado, it's all about the aubergine now – on our plates, around our homes and even in our wardrobes," announced *Stylist* magazine in a 2016 article entitled "Aubergine is the new black".

Purple has had its moments as it returned to fashion, usually on a wave of nostalgia for bygone eras, such as a 2005 revival of the Biba style of deep, earthy tones in vibrant prints. These included Prada's Spring 2005 ready-to-wear collection, with muted mauve shirts and aubergine minidresses worn with an array of clashing colours, like the psychedelic posters of the 1960s. For Alice Temperley's Autumn 2005 ready-to-wear collection, models were given soft-focus, 1970s-style purple eyeshadow, crimson and purple floral headbands over middle-parted hair, and plum-coloured knitted scarves. For designer Anna Sui, the Biba counter at Bergdorf Goodman in New York was a magical Aladdin's cave that inspired her own collections. "I used to come into New York from Michigan every summer," she recalled, "and I looked forward to the colors, the plums and teals and maroons that were murkier and more exciting than any color you had ever seen."

In Luca Guadagnino's 2009 film *I Am Love*, Tilda Swinton is an impeccably dressed wife and mother in Milan. Her elegant block-coloured wardrobe symbolizes her emotional journey, including a shift dress in striking plum wool, which hints at her deep desire for more passion.

While purple represents nostalgia, it also holds a sense of futurism. When the aubergine emoji first appeared in 2011, purple took on a new meaning as a phallic reference point, and as Instagram tried to ban the emoji because it was being used in an offensive way, the symbol developed a further subversive tinge. Purple has also been hailed as indicative of a superfood, with research from 2017 revealing the benefits of anthocyanins found in foods such as aubergine, purple cauliflower, elderberries and beetroot, leading to an interest in clothing and make-up that offered a healthy vibe.

The trend for purple tied in with fashion and make-up, with models at Dior's Autumn/Winter 2016 collection made up with dark and glossy plum-jam lips. For Givenchy's Autumn/Winter 2018/19 collection, Clare Waight Keller was inspired by a gritty, sleazy 1980s glamour. She created shimmering purple pleated gowns, which resembled the shape of shells and sea anemones, conjuring up thoughts of murex purple.

In 2018, Pantone's colour of the year was ultraviolet, which referenced the thoughts of the psychedelic era and the idea that the colour could offer creative inspiration by tapping into spirituality and taking awareness to a higher level. It was a colour that came to represent hope for the future, at a time that felt more politically charged and dangerous than ever.

The inauguration of President Joe Biden in January 2021 was a muted affair. Not only was it at the height of the Covid-19 pandemic, when huge crowds couldn't gather as they would normally in Washington, D.C., but also, America and the rest of the world was shaken by the storming of the U.S. Capitol building on 6 January. However, one thing that was evident that day was the sea of vivid block colours among the attendees, particularly purple. Vice President Kamala Harris wore a deep violet coat and dress by African American designer Christopher John Rogers, while Michelle Obama chose a wine-coloured ensemble of matching coat, turtleneck and wide-legged trousers. Hillary Clinton was dressed in her signature pantsuit in purple, and one of Jill Biden's outfits was a warm purple coat by independent New York designer Jonathan Cohen, with matching accessories. Purple was chosen as the colour of unity, blending the blue of the Democrats with the red of the Republicans, and was adopted symbolically by these Democratic women to indicate that Biden's new government heralded a sense of optimism after the tumultuous years of his predecessor Donald Trump.

Purple truly is a colour that transcends boundaries – from a colour used exclusively for royalty, to one that lit up the streets of London in violent shades of violet and mauve, and changed the course of science in the process. It can be both mournful or mystical and spiritual, quirky and expressive, and a colour that brings hope for uniting a country.

Tilda Swinton in a purple dress by Raf Simons for *I Am Love* (2009).

When Andy Sachs (played by Anne Hathaway) in *The Devil Wears Prada* (2006), smirks at the difficulty Meryl Streep's Miranda Priestly has in choosing between two apparently similar belts, the ice-cool fashion magazine editor reels off a monologue about the origins of Andy's "lumpy" cerulean blue sweater – a colour chosen by the very people in fashion who she mocks. "What you don't know is that that sweater is not just blue. It's not turquoise. It's not lapis. It's actually cerulean," she says, as she lists a number of designer collections the colour featured in, before it trickled down to department stores and discount shops. "It's sort of comical how you think you made a choice that exempts you from the fashion industry when, in fact, you're wearing a sweater that was selected for you by the people in this room, from a pile of stuff."

Blue

This piece of dialogue became one of the most memorable moments of the film, not only invoking the power of blue and its weighty history as a colour that people fought and died for, but because it helped to bring attention to cerulean, a shade that lies between azure and sky blue. Nominated by Pantone as the colour of the millennium in 1999 for its peaceful, tranquil qualities, the name derives from the Latin *caelum*, meaning "heaven" or "sky". Cerulean conjures up images of the Los Angeles swimming pools in David Hockney's paintings, and the photographs by Slim Aarons, where cool waters and blue skies evoke languorous pleasures.

In many cultures, blue connects the sky with the concept of heaven, where sky blue is known as *bleu celeste*, translated as "heavenly blue", in French. Hindu gods Krishna, Shiva and Rama all have blue auras and skin that connects them to the infinity of both the sky and the sea. For the ancient Egyptians, blue was the colour of the River Nile and the Egyptian god of the Universe, Amun-Ra, and when worn in jewellery, the hue was thought to dispel evil and bring prosperity.

Brilliant blue beads and necklaces were made using an artificial ultramarine, considered the oldest known synthetic pigment, originating around 3300 BCE. It was created from copper filings that were heated and combined with sand and potash, and was used for a wide range of decorative arts. The Egyptians called it *hsbd-iryt*, and the Romans referred to it as *caerulum* or "Egyptian blue".

While the Romans valued Egyptian blue for wall paintings and ceramics, blue clothing was rarely worn because they connected it to the barbarism of northern tribes. When Julius Caesar invaded Britain in 55 BCE, he described the ancient Scots, known as Picts, as painted blue. He said they "dye themselves with woad, which produces a blue colour, and makes their appearance in battle more terrible. They wear long hair, and shave every part of the body save the head and the upper lip."

Centuries later, blue transitioned from being an undervalued colour with negative connotations to one of the most beloved and prized. In the twentieth century, blue became the most requested colour for uniforms, from armed forces around the world, including the United States Navy and the Royal Air Force, to flight attendants and commercial pilots, as it conveyed stability and strength. As Sean Adams writes in *The Designer's Dictionary of Color* (2017): "If asked, most clients will suggest blue for a logo color. It communicates honesty and loyalty."

Indigo and woad

In the history of blue textiles, indigo plays a critical role, from the dyed threads of burial garments to the distinct wash of Levi's and Lee Rider jeans. As one of the most colourfast of dyes, the leaves of the *Indigofera tinctoria* have been utilized for over 6,000 years across Asia, Africa and the Americas. Indigo was a cornerstone of the transatlantic slave trade, helping to strengthen empires in Europe, and allowing plantations in the United States to thrive.

The oldest textile dyed with indigo dates from around 4200 BCE: a fragment of cotton fabric with blue stripes was uncovered at a burial site in Huaca, Peru in 2016. Before this discovery, it was believed the oldest indigo fabrics dated from 2400 BCE in ancient Egypt, where mummies were wrapped in blue-striped linen.

The word "indigo" derives from the Greek word *indikon* and the Latin word *indicum*, both meaning "from India", where indigo was first cultivated in the Indus Valley in north-west India, at least 5,000 years ago. For centuries, indigo was carried for thousands of miles along the Silk Road from India to Europe, in the form of crushed leaves rolled into balls, or as dried cakes created from the fermented leaves.

Dyeing with indigo is a complicated process. The leaves of the indigo plant are first soaked in water to break down the cells and release the pigment indigotin. To ensure the dye sticks to fabric, alkaline compounds like lime and wood ash are added to the mix. The oxygen in the vat must also be suppressed, and dyers traditionally did this by encouraging bacteria through the addition of sugary substances, but by the eighteenth century, dyers would introduce iron compounds. Many traditional recipes called for stale urine as a component of the dye bath to make it alkaline.

When the fabric is dipped into the vat, it initially emerges green, as the oxygen-free solution temporarily changes the pigment's chemical structure. But when it comes into contact with oxygen, the pigment turns a rich blue, and as the molecules expand, it sticks to the fibres of the material.

Before indigo found its way into Europe, blue dye was sourced from the native woad, *Isatis tinctoria*, a member of the cabbage family. Archaeological finds reveal that woad has been grown in Europe since the Neolithic age, around 8000 to 3000 BCE, when it was used as a paint and for clothing for northern Europeans. The long dye process was similar to that of indigo, where woad leaves were crushed and fermented for several weeks in urine, to make a paste that was shaped into round cakes for easy transportation.

Because the blue dye from woad was weaker than indigo and washed out easily, it was exempt from the sumptuary laws that dictated the rules of dress, and was reserved for the poor. It was, however, used as a base for creating blacks and purples when combined with red dye, or for greens, when combined with yellow. By the 1230s, woad was being produced on an industrial scale to meet demand from dyers.

The new fashion for blue in the Middle Ages was partly influenced by the twelfth-century depictions in art of the Virgin Mary in luminous blue robes, and was aided by the import of the precious rock lapis lazuli (ultramarine) from Afghanistan. Using one of the most expensive pigments –

worth more than gold – in stained-glass windows further glorified Mary, such as the cobalt blue glass of the Notre-Dame de la Belle Verrière of Chartres cathedral. It was also applied to works including the Wilton Diptych, painted for King Richard II, with Mary and 11 angels in ultramarine, also known as "Marian blue".

The use of lapis lazuli as a pigment coincided with dyers learning how to use woad effectively, and by the thirteenth century, blue rivalled red as the sought-after colour for European royals and aristocrats. Skilled Italian dyers of the Renaissance developed a range of different blue shades by experimenting with dyes and mordants, further aided by the arrival of indigo.

By the seventeenth century, Britain and France established indigo plantations in their colonies in the West Indies, further fuelling a trade in slave labour. Indigo had played an important role in West African culture since the eleventh century. For the Yoruba people, it was burned as incense to ward off bad spirits and was used as an antiseptic and a cosmetic enhancement for skin and hair. The Yoruba were known for their skills in cultivating and dyeing with indigo, and the women were particularly famed for their indigo-patterned *adire* cloths. In the Hausa kingdom of Kano, established around 1000 CE, lucrative indigo dye pits were controlled by the concubines of the royal household, who used indigo cloth as currency. For centuries, trade caravans loaded up with valued goods, including indigo and gold, were pulled by camels across the Sahara, and by the seventeenth century, they were leading 500 slaves at a time, to be taken to the coast and shipped to America's colonies.

The Tuareg people, a semi-nomadic group that have inhabited stretches of the Sahara for centuries, played the role of traders in these caravans. They have a longstanding tradition of wearing an indigo-dyed gauzy cotton *tagelmust*, also known as a *litham*, around their head and face. The

1. Ancient Egyptian pectoral, 5th–4th century BCE.

2. A member of the Tuareg tribe, Mali.

blue indigo powder, mixed with goat fat and beaten into the cloth, transferred from their clothes to their face and hands, leading to their nickname "the blue men".

When the Yoruba people were forcefully transported across the Atlantic, they carried with them their knowledge of growing, and dyeing with, indigo. South Carolina in the mid-1700s became a major indigo producer after Eliza Lucas, the 16-year-old daughter of a plantation owner, came across indigo seeds and soon discovered that her slaves had knowledge of producing the dye. Aware that indigo was in great demand for textiles in Europe, she convinced other farmers that they should cultivate it, and by the outbreak of the American Revolutionary War, South Carolina planters were exporting 1.1 million pounds of indigo into Europe. Indigo played such a vital role in the slave trade that American abolitionists and Quakers boycotted indigo and cotton fabric in their campaigns against slavery.

In the French courts of the eighteenth century, when indigo was being imported from the West Indian colonies, delicate blue was a favourite colour for elaborate gowns and decoration. Madame de Pompadour, the mistress of King Louis XV, frequently wore blue forget-me-not flowers in her hair and on her gowns as a symbol of faithfulness to the king. Marie Antoinette was similarly besotted with cornflower-blue silk for her *robes à la Française.* After Britain lost its foothold on America at the end of the American Revolution in 1783, it turned to India once again as the source of indigo production. The East India Company was brutal in its exploitation of local workers as factories across the Indian subcontinent created the blue-dyed fabrics for the British army's blue woollen greatcoats and sailor uniforms. The demand for indigo increased to such an extent that Indian farmers, particularly in the Bengal region, were forced to grow indigo instead of other crops, including staple foods. They were trapped in mounting debts that passed down generations, and which could never be cleared off given the low prices offered by the British Raj for indigo.

In 1859, in the Nadia district of Bengal, thousands of indigo farmers rose up against the repressive East India Company traders. The Indigo Revolt spread out to other villages before being violently suppressed by the military. An Indigo Commission was held in 1860 by the governing body of Bengal to look into the origins of the uprising, where it was said that "not a chest of indigo reached England without being stained with human blood".

Following William Perkin's discovery of aniline dyes in 1856, a German chemist named Adolf von Baeyer began developing a synthetic indigo, which he eventually achieved in 1880, after 14 years of research. By 1897, a commercially feasible dye was developed, which resulted in a dramatic drop in demand for natural indigo dye – from 19,000 tons in 1897 to 1,000 tons in 1914.

As the indigo market collapsed, the conditions of Indian farmers became even more desperate. Inspired by the Indigo Revolt, Mahatma Gandhi held his first acts of non-violent passive resistance in 1917 to speak out for enslaved indigo workers of Champaran, in the northern Bihar state. Gandhi's actions helped arouse public awareness, eventually leading to an overhaul of the treatment of indigo planters.

A new fashion for blue

Around 1705, a Swiss paint manufacturer, Johann Jacob Diesbach, stumbled across the first synthesized blue pigment when he was making up a cochineal red lake; a pigment rendered insoluble with the addition of iron sulphate and potash. When the batch turned pink, then purple and blue, he discovered the reaction had occurred because the potash was contaminated with a noxious substance known as "bone oil". He named his discovery

"Prussian blue", and it was immediately clear this could be the new Egyptian blue, the recipe of which had long been lost.

By 1750, Prussian blue was manufactured as a breakthrough textile dye for desirable teal shades, and was universally adopted for the uniforms of the mighty Prussian military. The new, moody blue pigment was quickly adopted by painters including Antoine Watteau, and a century later by the Japanese artist Katsushika Hokusai, for his iconic *The Great Wave off Kanagawa* (1830–32), and by Vincent van Gogh for *Starry Night* (1889).

The invention of Prussian blue led to a fever for blue-dyed clothing, and by the nineteenth century, natural and synthetic dyes were used for gowns in a variety of shades of blue. An aqua-blue dress with woven stripes, in the collection of the Victoria & Albert Museum, was worn by a woman called Isobella Bowhill to the International Exhibition of 1862, where the latest innovations in aniline dyes were showcased. London's parks and salons dazzled with brilliantly hued silk gowns, and blue was one of the most popular. Ranging from green-tinged turquoise to duck egg, cobalt, navy and midnight, blue was considered versatile for any season. In their 1870 book *Color in Dress*, authors William and George Audsley describe blue as "a cold and retiring color ... symbolical of divinity, intelligence, sincerity, and tenderness."

The discovery of electricity by Thomas Edison and Joseph Swan sparked a trend for electric blue, with the *Young Ladies' Journal* of February 1892 mentioning a dress of "electric-blue fancy brocade cloth". Considered the ultimate in modernity, electricity opened up countless new possibilities in technological innovations. Almost 150 years later, Timothée Chalamet became renowned as one of the most fashion-forward actors when he wore a shimmering electric-blue tunic and trousers, designed by Haider Ackermann, for the Sydney film premiere of *The King* in

October 2019. It referenced a tradition of blue suits for men, sparked by two artistic moments in the 1770s.

Blue for sorrow and for strength

In 1774, Johann Wolfgang von Goethe published his literary sensation *The Sorrows of Young Werther*, about a sensitive artist who is driven to suicide by his overwhelming unrequited love. Werther is described as wearing a blue tailcoat and a yellow waistcoat and breeches. On the back of the huge popularity of the story, young men began wearing their own versions of the blue coat. What's more, porcelain was decorated with scenes from the novel, a perfume (eau de Werther) was released and his costume featured in the pages of fashion books.

It was a phenomenon that became known as Werther Fever, and as one of the first "moral panics", the book was blamed for a wave of young suicides, leading to Copenhagen and Leipzig banning the wearing of the Werther blue coat. The book, and Werther's style, was particularly influential on the poets and artists of the Romantic movements, where blue was suited to the theme of sorrow. Goethe, who would explore his views on colour in his *Theory of Colours* in 1810, said, "We love to contemplate blue – not because it advances to us, but because it draws us after it."

One of the most recognizable blue suits in art is Thomas Gainsborough's 1770 painting *The Blue Boy*, which had originally been entitled *A Portrait of a Young Gentleman*. Infiltrating pop culture, the shimmering blue suit of the painting inspired a range of pastiche and parody, from F.W. Murnau's 1919 German expressionist film *The Boy in Blue*, where a young man believes he's the reincarnation of the boy in blue, to Austin Powers's camp blue velvet suit with frothy white collar and cuffs.

The blue suit was also memorably referenced in Quentin Tarantino's film *Django Unchained* (2012), where it

1. Jamie Foxx in Quentin Tarantino's *Django Unchained* (2012).

2. Timothée Chalamet at the Sydney, Australia premiere of *The King* in 2019.

conveyed the transformation of Django (Jamie Foxx) from captive to saviour, from wearing dehumanizing rags to the most resplendent fashion. Once he has freedom, he can express himself in the way that is true to him.

After escaping from slavery, Django chooses a blue velvet knickerbocker suit with a laced blouse, in a popular Victorian style known as "the Lord Fauntleroy suit". While the suit looks comical to the audience, particularly taking into account Jamie Foxx's own stylish and masculine persona off-screen, it also serves to make him visible in a world where his identity has been suppressed. The film's costume designer Sharen Davis said: "The blue valet suit is a liberty."

Kendra N. Bryant, in her essay "The Making of a Western-Negro-Superhero-Savior: Django's Blue Velvet Fauntleroy Suit", described *Django Unchained* as "just as politically righteous, flamboyantly beautiful, and disturbingly absurd as hip hop culture", wherein African Americans "wear flashy, fantastical clothing and accessories in order to announce their existence in a White patriarchal America that more often than not deems them invisible".

The abolitionist Olaudah Equiano, who settled in London after buying his freedom in 1766, described in his memoirs the power of a blue suit. Born in 1745 in the village of Essaka, in the Kingdom of Benin, and enslaved as a child, he was transported to the Caribbean, where he was bought by a Royal Navy officer. He described how he saved "above eight pounds of my money for a suit of super-fine blue cloaths to dance in at my freedom". With the chance to wear his blue suit, "the fair as well as the black people immediately styled me by a new appellation, to me the most desirable in the world, which was freeman."

In his memoirs, he hinted that his love of a blue suit came from the traditions of his homeland, where the men and women of Essaka wore a long piece of calico, or muslin, wrapped loosely round the body. "This is usually dyed blue, which is our favourite colour. It is extracted from a berry, and is brighter and richer than any I have seen in Europe," he wrote. The berry could be a reference to the species of indigo, *Philenoptera cyanescens*, also known as "Yoruba indigo", where both the fruit and leaves yield a blue dye.

As with the Romantic adoption of Werther's coat, blue is often considered to be the colour of sadness. Blue flags were raised on ships to indicate a captain or an officer had died on the voyage. By the end of the nineteenth century, African Americans had developed the "blues" as a form of music to express their emotional state. From there, the colour blue, in connection with music, indicated a sense of depression and internal anguish. Perhaps the blue of indigo, which, along with cotton, had kept Black people enslaved for centuries, was also an influence on the music.

True blue denims

Levi Strauss was a young German Jewish businessman who had arrived in New York at the age of 18. He travelled to California in 1853 to take advantage of the Gold Rush by selling products from his family's dry goods business to the pioneers heading west. One of Strauss's regular customers, a Nevada tailor called Jacob Davis, had begun making up popular work overalls for some of his customers from a durable cotton twill from Nîmes, France, which became known as *serge de Nîmes* or "denim". Davis approached his denim supplier, Strauss, with a proposition to go into business together, and in 1873 they obtained a patent for their hard-wearing "waist overalls", reinforced with copper rivets. Because of the difficulty in dyeing denim, Strauss chose a standard indigo blue from South Carolina, as it was cheaper and could withstand multiple washes without fading.

Indigo is crucial to the desirability of denim. Because denim is a twill-woven fabric with an undyed weft and indigo-dyed warp, the durable side is dyed, while the reverse is left almost white. As indigo fades over time, it creates a contrast with the white core of the thread. Douglas Luhanko and Kerstin Neumuller write in *Indigo*:

> The wear and tear on any denim garment gives an insight into what the person who was wearing the garment experienced ... Their life leaves its trace in the jeans, whether that life was of someone who was searching for happiness with a pick axe in 19th-century America or of a small child today, whose antics in the park tear holes in the knees.

Blue denims became a utilitarian tool for working on farms, on ranches and in mines, and by the beginning of the twentieth century, there were two other major competitors – Lee Jeans, and the Blue Bell Overall Company, later renamed Wrangler. Their popularity was driven by the westerns produced by Hollywood and then on television, and the 1930s trend for vacationing on stud ranches, creating a romanticized myth around the cowboy in his durable work clothes.

After the Second World War, jeans became imbued with countercultural symbolism as the uniform of the "blue-collar worker" was adopted by rebellious youths. It was what anthropologist Ted Polhemus referred to as an example of "dressing down", where the middle classes took on the dress of the working classes, who had worn practical blue for police, postal and transport uniforms, as well as denim on ranches.

In the film *Rebel without a Cause* (1955), James Dean wore his iconic red windbreaker and white T-shirt, with Lee 101Z Riders dipped in blue dye to make them pop even more in Technicolor. As part of his research, costume designer Moss Mabry spent several days at Los Angeles high schools, observing the clothes and styles of teenagers in jeans, resulting in the wardrobe department ageing more than 400 pairs of Levi's for the extras. "It was learned that high school boys who wear Levi's always try to dirty the pants first and then have them washed three or four times to get that well-worn look", said a publicity statement from Warner Brothers. As angst-ridden Jim Stark, James Dean spoke for an entire generation of young people, and his blue jeans, worn in all three of his movies before his untimely death in 1955, became their symbol.

From being associated with hard work and grit, and the pioneering spirit of cowboys, jeans were now associated with danger and sex, and led to a moral panic around rock 'n' roll and movies that depicted teenagers in denim. As Edgar Morin wrote in his 1960 book *The Stars: An Account of the Star-System in Motion Pictures*, James Dean "defined what one might call the panoply of adolescence, a wardrobe in which is expressed a whole attitude towards society: blue jeans, heavy sweaters, leather jacket, no tie, unbuttoned shirt, deliberate sloppiness are so many ostensible signs of a resistance against the social conventions of a world of adults." Women also poured themselves into blue jeans, with stars like Marilyn Monroe and Elizabeth Taylor imbuing them with a feminine sensuality as the denim clung to their curves.

From 1964 to 1975, Levi Strauss's sales grew from $100 million a year to $1 billion, as fabric suppliers struggled to keep up with shortages of indigo dye. In the Vietnam War era, shrink-to-fit jeans represented sexual liberation and freedom, tinged with urban and rock 'n' roll countercultural hipness. "It's a little strange to rise from work clothes to high fashion," the president of Levi Strauss, Peter E. Haas, said in 1973, "but we're not fighting it."

In the 1970s and 1980s, on the back of a rockabilly revival, jeans paired with denim jackets became a subversive, rebellious look once more, worn by Debbie Harry on stage in 1978. In 1984, the company launched

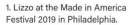

1. Lizzo at the Made in America Festival 2019 in Philadelphia.

2. James Dean on the set of *Giant*, 1955.

3. Women pilots of the Air Transport Auxiliary (ATA) in 1942. From left to right: Lettice Curtis, Jenny Broad, Wendy Sale Barker, Gabrielle Patterson and Pauline Gower.

its highly effective "501 Blues" television campaign, combining the azure hue of their jeans with popular blues music, boosting the brand's reputation as a hip label with a countercultural history, and leading to a steady climb of sales in the 1990s. During the grunge era of the early 1990s, blue denim was combined with crisp white and worn by stars like Drew Barrymore and Winona Ryder, as well as by Cindy Crawford in her 1992 Pepsi commercial, all furthering the simple sex appeal of denim.

The hot celebrity couple of the millennium, Britney Spears and Justin Timberlake, arrived at the 2001 American Music Awards dressed in matching all-denim outfits – Timberlake in a denim tuxedo and cowboy hat, and Spears in a strapless denim dress – believed at the time to be a stunt to mark their first public appearance as a couple. It was a moment where denim's cool factor imploded. "If you wear denim-on-denim, it will get documented. You know what, I don't think I could even bring that back," Timberlake later reflected.

On the back of a nostalgia for millennial style, with Lana Del Rey singing 'Blue Jeans' as an ode to a James Dean-esque lover, denim-on-denim was revived by designers in the 2010s, this time a little bit tongue-in-cheek. Katy Perry wore a Versace Couture denim gown at the 2014 Video Music Awards as an homage to Britney Spears, accompanied by hip-hop star Riff Raff dressed in the style of Timberlake, and Maria Grazia Chiuri combined distressed blue denim for jeans and jackets for her Spring/Summer 2018 ready-to-wear collection for Dior. Pop star Lizzo also embraced the double denim look with faded denim hot pants and bustier at the 2019 Made in America Festival.

From navy blue to Air Force blue
When fashion designer Mainbocher was commissioned to design the uniform for the WAVES, the female branch of the United States Navy during the Second World War,

his navy blue suits were so coveted that they led to an increase in applications to the service. For many women, it was their first chance to own a well-tailored garment designed by a renowned couturier, and the dark blue was considered much more attractive than the khaki of the Women's Army Corps, giving them a professional, stylish and efficient look and attitude.

Similarly, for the British female pilots of the Air Transport Auxiliary, their blue and gold jackets and skirts created a sense of dynamism, providing them with first-class service, such as the best tables in restaurants and seats on the bus, by those who spotted them in their uniforms. As ATA pilot Jackie Sorour recounted, when she tried on her "magnificent" uniform from Moss Brothers: "Quite suddenly I realized that I was not bad looking ... For the first time in my life heads turned as I walked along the street."

The uniform's shade of blue referenced the colours of the RAF; it was a high-status uniform which stood out from the khaki-clad British Army, members of which were insultingly referred to as "brown jobs." RAF hero Colin "Hoppy" Hodgkinson, who lost both legs in an air accident in 1938, felt rehabilitated when he was posted into 131 Squadron in 1942. He wrote in his autobiography: "Air Force Blue, at that time the most famous colour in the world ... I smoothed the wings above my left breast pocket, prinked like a mannequin up and down before a glass. My God! Nothing could stop me now. I was irresistible!"

One of the most coveted uniforms for women outside of wartime was for Pan Am flight attendants, who were treated like stars as they arrived at hotels around the world. When Pan Am hired its first seven stewardesses in 1944, Smith, Gray & Company designed the uniform with the pale blue known as "Tunis Blue", after Elizabeth Tunis, Pan Am's first chief stewardess. Such was the prestige of the stewardess uniform that legendary Hollywood fashion designer Howard Greer was commissioned to design a Transcontinental & Western uniform in 1944, choosing a pale grey-blue, and Cristóbal Balenciaga was commissioned to design a navy blue woollen serge jacket and skirt for Air France in 1969. That same year, Evan Picone redesigned the Pan Am uniform to create a riding jacket, skirt and bowler hat in "Superjet blue" to herald the arrival of the first 747. The Pan Am uniforms perfectly summed up the glamour of the jet age, matching the company logo of a hemispheric globe, showing the earth without boundaries.

The blue of the horizon

With her long blonde hair capped with a headband, wearing a sky-blue dress with a white apron, long socks and Mary Janes, the heroine of Lewis Carroll's *Alice's Adventures in Wonderland* (1865) is one of literature's most instantly recognizable characters. In her journey down the rabbit hole, her costume not only marks her out as a young girl, but it signifies the potential in her life as she steps outside of her boundaries and explores this "curious and curiouser" new world.

Alice wasn't always in blue – she wore a yellow dress in the colour illustrations done by E. Gertrude Thomson for Carroll's shortened version of the story for children, called *The Nursery "Alice"*, in 1890 – but by 1911, when Macmillan published 16 new colour plates by Harry Theaker, blue would be the pervading colour for Alice's dress. For the 1951 Disney adaptation, artist Mary Blair designed her butter-blonde Alice in a contemporary New Look silhouette. She shaded the dress a colour already known as "Alice blue" – after President Roosevelt's daughter Alice Roosevelt – which had inspired a hit song, 'Alice Blue Gown', in 1919. Thanks to the popularity of Disney's version, the dreamy Alice in blue was firmly established. The little-girl innocence of Alice's blue dress was, however, given a sinister twist in Stanley Kubrick's

The Shining (1980), with the matching outfits of the haunting Grady Twins, making them even more terrifying.

In 2003, *Vogue* commissioned Annie Leibovitz to shoot model Natalia Vodianova in 11 specially commissioned blue dresses for a 22-page Alice-themed spread, where Vodianova, as Alice, posed next to the designers in a series of photographs inspired by Wonderland. These included a Viktor&Rolf multilayered silk dress, a blue Christian Lacroix confection for the Mad Hatter's tea party, and a Tom Ford for Yves Saint Laurent Rive Gauche sky-blue silk satin dress.

That same year, Gwen Stefani punked up Alice with her 'What You Waiting For?' music video, in custom-made John Galliano and Vivienne Westwood powder-blue corsets and tiny bustle skirts. Stefani's concept for her album *Love. Angel. Music. Baby.* controversially borrowed from the fashions of the Lolita subculture of Japan, which was in turn inspired by frilly Alice in Wonderland Victoriana. The record was Stefani's first as a solo artist after a decade in the band No Doubt, and the overarching theme of the song explored her hesitancy in going solo; this brave step into the unknown was further symbolized by the sky blue of her Alice-inspired costumes.

While boys are so often associated with blue, adventurous girls in literature, animations and film are often depicted wearing a blue dress as they step outside their comfort zones, to find a sense of freedom and adventure. Blue, the colour of the infinite sky, indicates their potential, that they can explore beyond the borders of the world they already inhabit. Similarly, another famous blue dress is the gingham frock worn by Dorothy in *The Wizard of Oz* (1939), as she is transported from sepia-tinted Kansas to the Technicolor Land of Oz. Costume designer Adrian's challenge was to make the 17-year-old Judy Garland appear younger, and so he chose a blue gingham material he had sourced in Appalachia for a costume that marked her out as a girl on a journey.

In Disney's *Beauty and the Beast*, Belle is a voracious reader – it's her only means of exploring a world outside her small French village. Her blue peasant dress, worn over a white smock, and with a white apron, is symbolic of a new life waiting for her. In the live-action 2017 version, Jacqueline Durran designed Emma Watson's costumes based on the original designs for the 1990 animation. "There is a sort of refinement and crispness to light blue, but there's also blue in workwear," she said. "It is a practical color, and a color that you can work in. In that sense, it is full of active strength."

Grace Kelly wore an ice-blue duchess satin gown to the Academy Awards in 1955 when she pipped Judy Garland to the Best Actress Oscar for *The Country Girl*. Her gown was considered the highlight of the ceremony, with gossip columnist Hedda Hopper describing her in the *Los Angeles Times* as "like a dream walking". It was designed by Paramount Pictures' costume designer Edith Head, and Kelly recounted to *Photoplay* in 1955 that she had "wanted something blue" to wear. Head had previously dressed Kelly in a Delphi-inspired sky-blue chiffon gown for Alfred Hitchcock's *To Catch a Thief* (1955), which fitted with the trend for Grecian gowns in the 1950s, and served to highlight her as a favourite glacial "Hitchcock blonde". The dress could also be indicative of her character Francie's desire to expand her horizons, as she finds excitement in helping to catch a jewel thief targeting the wealthy on the Côte d'Azur.

Another woman bound for more was the character Ally in *A Star is Born* (2018). For the emotional finale, the costume designer, Erin Benach, created a custom-made gown described as "robin's-egg blue" as Ally performs 'I'll Never Love Again'. The inspiration was Grace Kelly's 1955 Academy Awards dress, because it was simple, but impactful, and wouldn't take away from the punch of that final scene. "We knew this was the emotional apex of the

1. The Grady Twins in Stanley Kubrick's *The Shining* (1980).

2. Lady Gaga in Valentino at the 76th Annual Golden Globe Awards in 2019.

3. Grace Kelly in Alfred Hitchcock's *To Catch a Thief* (1955), in a gown by Edith Head.

1. Givenchy, S/S 2018.

2. Dolce and Gabbana, A/W 2016 – inspired by *Alice in Wonderland*.

movie and as soon as you put a really strong design on her, it just took away from the moment," said Benach. The colour of the dress also harked back to a periwinkle-blue ball gown worn by Judy Garland in the 1954 version of the film, marking a moment when she reaches the horizon of the stardom she's been seeking. This was referenced again in the periwinkle dress worn by Gaga when she collected a Golden Globe in 2019 for the song 'Shallow', written for the 2018 version of the movie.

Rebecca Solnit's 2005 essay "Yves Klein and the Blue of Distance" examined the artist Yves Klein's spiritual use of blue, as the colour of the "spirit, the sky, and water, the immaterial and the remote". Klein patented a shade known as "International Klein Blue", which heralded his blue period, beginning in 1957. Like the Pan Am logo, his blue globe depicted a world where boundaries created by humans had been eradicated. Solnit further elaborated on the transcendence of blue in her 2005 book *A Field Guide to Getting Lost:*

> ... the blue at the horizon, the blue of land that seems to be dissolving into the sky, is a deeper, dreamier, melancholy blue, the blue at the farthest reaches of the places where you see for miles, the blue of distance. This light that does not touch us, does not travel the whole distance, the light that gets lost, gives us the beauty of the world, so much of which is in the color blue.

Despite its connection to sorrowful emotions, blue is a colour that is considered loyal, true and calm, as it represents that space between the sky and the sea. Perhaps that's why it's so often chosen as a favourite colour.

With interpretations ranging from sexuality and fantasy to devilish temptation and toxicity, green can be a startling choice of colour to wear. It's glamorous, but with an edge – hinting at danger and seduction, or implying a contrast between vitality and death. While dusky eau-de-Nil satins and emerald-hued velvets evoke luxury and style, one of green's strongest links is to nature, health, forests and gardens. As naturalist John Muir once said, "Nature in her green, tranquil woods heals and soothes all afflictions," and when we surround ourselves with green, it can act as a balm to the soul.

Green

"Green is the colour of balance and harmony," writes Karen Haller in 2019's *The Little Book of Colour*. "It sits between the physicality of red, the intellect of blue and the emotion of yellow. In essence, green is the balance between the mind, body and emotional self." When we see green, we know that there will be water and life to sustain us, and plenty of oxygen from plants and trees to clear our heads and allow us to breathe. But it also represents death and decay when we think of green mould, or of poison and toxicity.

This association of green with nature goes back to classical times. In ancient Egypt, green was the colour of regeneration and growth and it was commonly represented by the hieroglyph of a papyrus sprout. A paint palette containing malachite, a copper carbonate pigment, was discovered in Tutankhamen's tomb, indicating that green powder was painted around the eyes of the living and the dead, as a symbol of rebirth and to protect from evil.

The Romans also made a connection with the colour green and the bloom of the natural world. Green was chosen to represent Venus, goddess of gardens, vegetables and vineyards, and the Latin word for green, *viridis*, also translates to "young", "fresh", "lively" or "youthful". In Islamic countries, the colour green holds significance for its life-giving properties. Green was the colour of the Prophet Muhammad, and those in paradise were described in the Quran as being dressed in "green garments of fine silk", as they were blissfully surrounded by the greenery of pleasure gardens.

Medieval myths of green
Hiding out in Sherwood Forest to escape the law, Robin Hood and his band of Merry Men were, from their earliest depictions, swathed in clothing coloured Lincoln green. The folk ballad *A Gest of Robyn Hode*, written around 1450, described how "when they were clothed in Lyncolne grene they kest away their gray", indicating that lush green hues

were more uplifting than the dull browns and greys that peasants normally wore.

Medieval painters often used green to represent the clothing of huntsmen, as a form of camouflage that allowed them to blend into the woodland and vegetation. Robin Hood's leafy hued garments symbolized the way they sought safety by hiding under the cover of Sherwood Forest. While much of the legend of Robin Hood was told in ballads and steeped in myth, Lincoln green was indeed a popular fabric in the Middle Ages, along with the more expensive Lincoln scarlet. The shade was named for the skilful dyers of Lincoln, a major cloth-manufacturing centre, who dipped fabric into vats of blue woad, followed by yellow weld, to create a natural green.

Green was notoriously difficult to achieve when it came to pigments and dyes, and so the colour was often overlooked in favour of more brilliant hues, such as red and blue, which could be achieved with madder and woad or indigo. Green cloth was traditionally dyed with the natural juices of plants like fern, plantain, nettles, leeks, and the bark of the alder tree, yet they faded quickly and the colour didn't stay. Woad overdyed with weld was the way to achieve a strong green, but during the Middle Ages, a taboo developed around the mixing of dyes.

Strict regulations of the textile industries by guilds across Europe forbade the combining of dyes together to achieve compound colours. Dyers were given licences to work within certain parameters, such as only with black or blue dyes, to ensure the correct processes were followed for a high-quality product. In order to crack down on any contravention to these rules, the mixing of dyes was declared a "demonic operation". In some countries, anyone caught dyeing with woad and weld to create green cloth could be given large fines or even forced into exile, as in the case of German dyer Hans Töllner in 1386. By 1600,

Lincoln green had been resigned to history and myth, with Elizabethan poet Michael Drayton writing in "Poly-Olbion" (1612) that "Lincoln anciently dyed the best green in England".

The taboo against mixing began to ease during the fifteenth and sixteenth centuries, when there were technical differences – and prices – between the dyeing processes for creating a vivid green from mixing versus a faded colour from vegetable dyes. By 1500, the town of Kendal in Cumbria was famous for its mass-manufacturing of a dull green wool, which was dyed with greenweed (dyer's broom) and then dipped in woad or indigo. Two centuries later, the fashion switched to the brighter Saxon green, which was created by mixing indigo and fustic, a tree dye also known as dyer's mulberry, which was one of the most popular yellow dyes in Europe at the time.

Renaissance painters found that green pigment was an unstable colour when applied to a surface, either fading quickly, or turning brown. Because it was so difficult to achieve a strong green shade in both fabric and in paintings, the colour began to signify the wealth and status of merchants and their families. In *The Arnolfini Portrait* (1434) by Jan van Eyck, the wife's green dress shows both the wealth of the family as well as symbolizing her fertility. While it appears that she's heavily pregnant, on closer inspection, she's holding up yards of green fabric against her body to display their riches.

To paint this striking green cloth, Van Eyck used verdigris, a substance that forms on old copper and creates a complex, unstable pigment. When applied, verdigris often fades to brown upon contact with other pigments, and it took great skill to ensure the green on the dress stayed as vivid as possible. While painters like Tintoretto struggled with it, Van Eyck developed a reputation as a magician of colour with his skilful application.

1. *Veronica Veronese* (1872) by Dante Gabriel Rossetti.

2. Evening dress by Charles Worth, 1887.

3. Jan Van Eyck's *Portrait of Giovanni Arnolfini and His Wife (The Arnolfini Marriage)* (1434).

Emerald green to die for

Madame Dominique, the top seamstress at the House of Chanel, spoke in a 2005 documentary, *Signé Chanel*, of how "seamstresses don't like green". Despite the huge popularity of green clothing over the last couple of centuries, there have also been lingering superstitions and insinuations of the colour being unlucky and devilish. This was because it was literally to die for, as the synthetic chemicals of the nineteenth century that created a strikingly vibrant green, such as Scheele's green and Paris green, contained high levels of arsenic that seeped into the wearers' and dressmakers' pores.

The story of green dye took a dramatic turn in 1775 when Carl Wilhelm Scheele, a Swedish scientist, discovered the compound copper arsenite while studying the properties of arsenic. After pouring potassium and white arsenic on a solution of copper vitriol, he knew he'd hit on a brilliant and powerful pigment. It was immediately sought-after for clothing and wallpapers, artificial flowers and even emerald-tinged sweets and blancmange. Scheele was well aware that his discovery could be poisonous, even writing to a friend about his concerns in 1777, but these evident dangers were brushed off by manufacturers of synthetic dyes, who thought only of the commercial possibilities. Scheele himself was killed by chemical poisoning only a decade later.

With the invention in 1814 of Paris green, another copper- and arsenic-based pigment emerald hues were now all the rage. Every wealthy woman with fashion credentials wore a green dress, shimmering like an expensive jewel. Green was not only linked with wealth and luxurious taste, but also tied to nature and health. During the Romantic movement in literature and art, established from the mid eighteenth century, artists like John Constable painted rich and fertile green landscapes as a respite from the smoggy cityscapes of the Industrial Revolution. People began to see the benefits of physical activity and fresh air, and zesty fabrics were the calming colour of choice. Another very popular mid-nineteenth-century fashion were elaborate wreaths for the hair, with foliage entwined with succulent-looking fruits and flowers. It was a trend sparked by 36-year-old Queen Victoria, when she was depicted in a watercolour by court artist Franz Xaver Winterhalter with a garland of leaves and flowers. Designers like Madame Tilman of Paris, mentioned in *Godey's Lady's Book*, Volume 52 in 1856 for her "artistic taste", kept up with the demand for green hair ornaments by employing thousands of workers in their cramped ateliers. By the 1850s, there were reports of the women and men who handled green dye suffering from agonizing sores on their fingers and arms, nausea, anaemia and pounding headaches. As for the elegant women who wore green dresses, they suffered skin irritation around their necklines and shoulders, or wherever fabric touched the skin.

It wasn't just clothing that was proving lethal. In Bradford, West Yorkshire, in 1858, 21 people were killed after eating green sweets dyed with arsenic that had been sold in a market stall by the miserly sounding "Humbug Billie". Another tragic case that hit the news was the death of Matilda Scheurer, an artificial flower-maker in London, whose job was to dust fashionable hair ornaments with a green powder to make them even more brilliant in colour. Scheurer's death in 1861 was reported in distressing detail – the whites of her eyes were tinged green, as was her vision, she vomited up green water, and finally, as she succumbed, she foamed at the mouth and nose as her internal organs gave up the fight.

Medics, suspicious about the number of similar cases they were coming across, began to test green-dyed fabrics and wallpapers, only to find that they contained high levels of arsenic. In February 1862, *Punch* magazine reflected on the sweeping fear of green, with its cartoon of two skeletons at a ball: a gentleman in tuxedo, and a woman in crinoline and toxic hair garland, with the headline "The Arsenic

Waltz: The new dance of death". Another satirical article in *Punch* suggested that women who wore green should be brandished with scarlet letters: "We think a man would be as green as the dress of his fair partner, if he either waltzed or polked with a lady in Scheele's green. In fact, girls in these green dresses ought to be marked 'DANGEROUS!' or to have 'BEWARE OF POISON!' embroidered in red letters right across their backs."

In 1862, it was reported that a number of ballerinas performing *Ondine* in Hamburg fell ill from the green of their ballet dresses. There was an article, in the *Southampton Herald* in February of that same year, entitled "The use of dresses and wreaths containing arsenic". It said:

> The brilliant greens which are produced from this noxious mineral have been so much admired by the votaries of dress, that their manufacture has been unduly stimulated, and large numbers of young women and children have been pressed into the service. The powder is of so volatile a character that the air of the room becomes impregnated with it, and particles of this deadly poison are inhaled at every inspiration ... the brightness of the colours produced does but enhance the misery of the toil. These lustrous leaves seem to mock the makers. They speak of beauty, gaiety, and mirth. But every glistening spray is an index of days shortened ... and of scenes of misery which cannot be described.

In the 1860s, there was no one more fashionable than Empress Eugénie, the beautiful Spanish-born wife of Napoleon III, whose every whim set international trends. In September 1863, she chose to wear an emerald-green silk gown to the Paris Opera, which had been coloured by a new, non-toxic aniline green dye, known as *vert Guignet*, or "viridian" in English. With a sprinkle of her custom gold dust in her hair, she made headlines the next morning for the way her gown had retained its vivacity and sheen under the newly invented gas lights. Following reports of Eugénie and her safer gown, women in Paris and London were desperate to wear a shimmering silk gown in *nouveau vert*. Charles Worth, the premier fashion designer of the late nineteenth century, created stunning pieces of haute couture in rich greens made from arsenic-free dyes, such as an 1887 ballgown, which featured a striking chartreuse silk bodice, bustle and train.

There had also been a number of campaigns from social reformers, such as The Ladies' Sanitary Association, to protect the factory workers who were toiling in dangerous environments to keep up with the demand for fashionable – and toxic – green fabrics and decorations. Yet women continued to wear "arsenic" green, because it was much more affordable, and more vivid, than the safe version.

As the founder of the Arts and Crafts movement, William Morris rejected machine-based mass production, including synthetic dyes, and sought for a nostalgic return to the natural, plant-based dyes of the past. His intricate patterns were inspired by nature, using a dominant palette of greens, from eau de Nil to rich evergreen. Morris purchased Merton Abbey Mills, a Surrey textile works, in 1881, where he created his fabric and wallpaper from traditional mineral and vegetable dyes, supposedly eschewing the latest synthetics. He invited visitors to Merton, where he delighted in demonstrating the traditional method of dipping wool dipped into vats of woad, followed by weld, showing them how the wool changed from the colour of grass to deep green and blue.

Despite William Morris's outspoken preference for natural dyes, a researcher at the University of Aberdeen named Andy Meharg discovered in 2003 that there were traces of arsenic in a sample of Morris's printed wallpaper, produced between 1864 and 1875. Morris was aware of the dangers, being a shareholder in his father's copper-mining company, Devon Great Consols, which was the largest arsenic producer of the time. Yet he dismissed public concern about green dyes, writing in a letter in 1885: "a greater folly is hardly possible to imagine: the doctors were bitten by witch fever." When it came to his own wallpapers, the natural dyes he championed just wouldn't convey a bright enough green for his swirling vine and leaf prints that decorated London's finest reception rooms.

With widespread fears of green's toxicity, the continual invention of safer dyes helped to democratize the colour throughout Europe and the United States. By the 1890s, green was everywhere – as a block colour or in vivid stripes. A black silk bodice and skirt with green and pink stripes, from the Parisian haute couture house Robina in 1892, and now part of the collection of the Art Institute of Chicago, demonstrates the passion for fashionable green. *Ladies' Home Journal* predicted in 1892: "Everything this season must be trimmed with lace, ribbon, and jet to give it the desired stylish air … every tint of green from light Nile to the moss shade, is fancied in Paris."

While arsenic green is thankfully relegated to the past, Alison Matthews David notes in *Fashion Victims* (2015) that one of the most popular greens in use today is a chemical dye known as malachite green, which was first synthesized in 1877. Malachite, derived from copper, was used throughout the nineteenth century for paint, and the dye is used regularly to tint textiles and leathers. It has been banned for use in food in North America and the European Union following studies that revealed it was harmful when consumed. "Despite the fact that it symbolizes nature and brands the ecological Green Movement, green was, and still is, among the most toxic colours to produce," writes Matthews David.

Absinthe and the green fairy

When Henri de Toulouse-Lautrec positioned himself at one of the tables of the newly opened Moulin Rouge in Montmartre in 1889 to sketch the whirl of colourfully dressed dancers and oddball customers, he was fuelled by glass after glass of absinthe. Sometimes he combined it with cognac, or simply took it served with a flambéed sugar cube, slowly doused in water until it dissolved into the milky jade liquid. Once Lautrec was woozy with intoxication, he often felt haunted by the green fairy, a little sprite in an emerald dress, who was said to come to absinthe drinkers in their hallucinations.

She was the symbol of the spirit, often depicted in paintings such as Albert Maignan's *Green Muse* (1895), or in advertising posters for brands of absinthe, draped in green. Lautrec felt like he was under the spell of absinthe's green as it fuelled his creativity, capturing the seedy side of Belle Époque Paris. "To me, in the colour green, there is something like the temptation of the devil", he said.

It was from the twelfth century that green began to be associated with the devil and his creatures across Europe; previously, Satan had been hideously represented by black for darkness and red for fire. In Michael Pacher's fifteenth-century painting *Saint Wolfgang and the Devil*, for example, the devil is depicted with menacing green skin. According to Michel Pastoureau in his 2014 study of the colour green, there was a sixteenth century saying that went: "grey eyes to paradise, black eyes to purgatory, green eyes to hell".

The Montmartre and Pigalle districts of Paris in the late nineteenth century were awash with absinthe, and the green fairy represented the potency of the districts' signature drink, where it didn't just make people drunk, but drove them mad. Distilled from wormwood, aniseed, fennel and wild marjoram, it was first associated with bohemians and artists like Vincent van Gogh, Oscar Wilde and Paul Gauguin, and by the 1870s it counted for 90 per cent of

1. Advert for Absinthe Blanqui, 1895.

2. *Young Lady with Gloves* (1930) by Tamara de Lempicka.

spirit consumption. Whole districts of Paris were said to smell of the herbal aroma in the early evening, a time known as *l'heure verte*, or "the green hour". Belle Époque artists like Lautrec were creating new forms of art, depicting the underbelly of the city in art nouveau posters and pamphlets. As well as the green fairy, adverts for absinthe during this time depicted red-haired women swathed in green Renaissance-style gowns as they raised a glass of the potent liquid, representing decadence and licentiousness. Vincent van Gogh was inspired by green, and its complimentary colour red, when creating his absinthe-tinged 1888 work *The Night Café*: "I sought to express with red and green the terrible human passions ... Everywhere it is a battle and antithesis of the most different reds and greens."

The red-haired heroines of Pre-Raphaelite painter and aesthete Dante Gabriel Rossetti owed a similarity to the women in the absinthe posters. Just as these art nouveau images referenced the Renaissance period, Rossetti's models were frequently dressed in voluminous robes in sage green, such as Alexa Wilding posing longingly in green velvet in *Veronica Veronese* (1872). William Morris's wife, Jane Morris, was the muse and lover of Rossetti, and in *The Day Dream* (1880), her loose green dress connects her to the nature that surrounds her and imbues her with a verdant sensuality.

The infamy of absinthe, and its illicitness, soon led to it being considered a green menace and placed it at the centre of a moral panic. In May 1868, *The Times* warned of the "emerald-tinted poison" that was causing so much addiction and death. By the outbreak of the First World War, absinthe had been banned in France, to ensure there was an effective, capable army who weren't driven to distraction by drink. While the green-tinged drink was demonized across Europe, it further accentuated the long-held notion of green as the colour of poison, of danger and of sex. This was particularly true of the decadent

1920s, when Jeanne Lanvin's chartreuse flapper dresses, produced from 1925, conveyed dangerous glamour.

Temptation, love, and *Atonement*

Green has a deep history of representing tempestuous love and illicit affairs. *Greensleeves*, a classic English folk song of the Elizabethan era, has been interpreted as being about a promiscuous woman, Lady Green Sleeves, where the green of her dress was said to hint that she was a sex worker. In ancient China, the husband of a prostitute wore a green headscarf, creating the expression "the family of the green lantern". Even today, people should take care in China wearing green hats, as they still hold those derogatory connotations.

As well as the illicit, green can also represent beauty and strong sensuality. In Tamara Lempicka's *Young Lady with Gloves* (1930), the emerald-green dress heightens the power of her sexuality by clinging tightly to her body, while her auburn hair matches those of the women in the Belle Époque absinthe posters. And think of Jennifer Lopez in green Versace, slashed to her navel, with a suggestion of rejuvenation in the lush jungle print, and of sensuality with the sheer fabric. There were so many internet searches for pictures of Lopez in this attention-grabbing dress that it led to the invention of Google Images in 2001.

One of the most talked about green dresses in recent years was a slip of emerald-green satin, worn by Keira Knightley in the film *Atonement* in 2007. She was a striking image in the risqué, silken Jean Harlow–style creation, which was both glamorous and nostalgic, representing a lost summer in the 1930s. The green silk fabric is barely there as it skims over her body, dipping right down to the base of her spine – the perfect dress for a "perfectly" remembered 1930s summer evening before the war. In Ian McEwan's novel on which the film was based, Cecelia pulls the gown from her wardrobe and slips it on, letting the

1. Keira Knightley in *Atonement* (2007).

2. Jennifer Lopez in Versace at the 2000 Grammy Awards.

hem fall to the floor. McEwan described her as a "mermaid" in the gown, linking green to the themes of water in the story, from the fateful fountain scene to Cecelia's watery death. The slinky green dress is much like the one worn by the eponymous Mrs Dalloway in Virginia Woolf's 1925 novel, where she glides through the party in a "silver-green mermaid's dress" with "the perfect ease and air of a creature floating in its element". Ultimately, the *Atonement* dress represents both a longing for flawless days of the past and allure and enticement. As the film's costume designer, Jacqueline Durran, said in a 2007 interview, "I think of green as temptation..."

Green is the colour of the serpent in the Garden of Eden who tempts Eve into taking a bite of the apple, leading to the fall of man. It's also associated with envy, as embodied by the expression "the green-eyed monster", which has been attributed as first coined by Shakespeare in *Othello* (1603). In the Middle Ages, green eyes were said to reveal a deceitful character, representing traitors, prostitutes and witches, and on stage and in paintings, duplicitous biblical characters like Judas and Delilah were often depicted in green.

Green is representative of water, and what lurks there was likely to be dangerous, too. Green frogs were considered slimy, as well as a symbol of lust (as suggested in the fairytale of *The Princess and the Frog*). The siren of mythology was a dangerous half-woman with an aqueous green fish-like tail, who could lure sailors to their death. The medieval tale of *Ondine* is a love story between a water nymph and a knight, and Ondine's dress in paintings and in stage productions is often tinged with green, as if she is an apparition from another world, dripping in seaweed. Green was similarly used in abundance by Pre-Raphaelite painters like Sir Edward Burne-Jones, who depicted fairies and sprites in green clothing, such as with *Green Summer* (1864), and Sir John Everett Millais's *Ophelia* (1851–52), where the green of life and growth contrasts with the dying Ophelia submerged in water, much like Cecelia's tragic watery death.

As well as for water, green also represents decay. Everything Gwyneth Paltrow wears in *Great Expectations* (1998) as Estella is a shade of green – a colour that infatuated director Alfonso Cuarón. Donna Karan provided several outfits for Paltrow, including a green velvet dress and a moss-green cardigan and skirt. Green is poisonous and decomposing, like the mansion of Miss Havisham, and it shows the untrustworthiness of Estella as a character.

The green light and the American dream
In F. Scott Fitzgerald's *The Great Gatsby* (1925), Nick first sees Jay Gatsby reaching out to a green light at the end of Daisy's dock, on the other side of the bay from him. The green light is what Gatsby strives for in life; it represents his yearning for Daisy and his desire to achieve the American dream. In countless depictions in books and films, green takes on a fantasy element, where it has come to represent wish fulfilment and the pursuit of dreams.

Emma Stone in *La La Land* (2016) wears an evergreen dress as she and Ryan Gosling soar among a glittering backdrop of stars at Griffith Observatory. The colour of the dress was specifically mentioned in the script, as green represents their wish for stardom, just as their faces are bathed in green light as they sing 'City of Stars' together. This dress, created by the film's costume designer Mary Zophres, was inspired by a dark green dress worn by Judy Garland in *Easter Parade* (1948), similarly about a young hopeful striving to achieve success.

In *Singin' in the Rain* (1952), the costumes we remember aren't necessarily the goody-two-shoes dresses of Debbie Reynolds, but rather the absinthe-hued flapper dress and matching heels worn by vampish Cyd Charisse in the "Broadway Melody" sequence, as she seduces Gene Kelly with a flex of her leg. This sequence was an elaborate fantasy piece, a 13-minute ballet about following your dreams, and Charisse is the unobtainable seductress. Charisse's green dress not only stands out against the ruby-red background, Kelly's banana-yellow vest, and the pink and orange dresses of the other dancers, but it creates a feeling of illicit sexuality as she guides him towards stardom, all the while remaining out of reach.

Eau de Nil was a shade of green that perhaps defined the decadence of the Golden Age of Hollywood. In the 1920s, the art deco movement looked to the exoticism of Eastern arts and took inspiration from ancient Egypt with fabric the colour of the silty waters of the Nile. Paul Poiret's "Arrow of Gold" dress, for example, created from green chiffon with threaded gilt arrows in 1925, perfectly encapsulated the Egyptian influence. The trend for eau de Nil made its way to Hollywood, and then back to ancient Egypt, for Claudette Colbert's costumes in 1934's *Cleopatra*. Costume designer Travis Banton aligned his designs with the art deco fashion for bias-cut satin gowns, including a shimmering mermaid-style gown in eau-de-Nil satin, with dramatic draped sleeves. It may not have been authentic to the real Cleopatra, but 1930s audiences lapped it up, and it inspired countless imitations in department stores.

Director Alfred Hitchcock was very much aware of the significance of colour when plotting out the costumes for his films, and eau de Nil was a particular favourite. As well as complementing the blonde hair of cool heroines, it was a neutral colour that wouldn't distract the audience during moments of tension on screen. This was why his costume designer Edith Head created a pale green dress and jacket for Tippi Hedren in *The Birds* (1963), which becomes increasingly sullied as the action unfolds. Head also designed an eau-de-Nil suit for Grace Kelly in *Rear Window* (1954), establishing her character as an impeccably dressed businesswoman. She once said: "Unless there is a story reason for a colour, we keep the colours muted, because

Hitchcock believes they can detract from an important action scene. He uses colour, actually, almost like an artist, preferring soft greens and cool colours for certain moods."

It was in Hitchcock's 1958 film *Vertigo* that he fully embraced green for symbolic effect. Jade green represents the mysterious character of Madeleine, played by Kim Novak, as she haunts the imagination of James Stewart's character, Scottie, like a ghost from the past. We first see Madeleine swathed in an emerald-green cloak, which clashes with the red, womb-like restaurant in much the same way as Van Gogh's *The Night Café*. When Scottie meets Judy, who has been pretending to be Madeleine as part of an elaborate scheme, she wears a mossy-green sweater and skirt, which reminds us, and Scottie, of Madeleine. Later, after Scottie obsessively transforms Judy into Madeleine, green light comes through her hotel window, bathing her in a supernatural glow. Hitchcock connected the green light to the London stage of his youth, recollecting fondly "the green light – green for the appearances of ghosts and villains".

From hippies to millennials

When the hippie subculture swept through America and Europe in the late 1960s and early 1970s, it was a wake-up call to fight for civil rights and to push environmental concerns to the forefront. In 1972, when the *Apollo 17* crew blasted into space for NASA's final moon-landing mission, they brought home with them the iconic photo of Planet Earth, known as *The Blue Marble*. It was the first time that people could truly appreciate the beauty of the green and blues of the planet. That same year, a group called Don't Make the Waves Committee changed its name to Greenpeace, and the UK's Green Party was officially launched, beginning the alignment of the colour green with a political movement.

A devastating oil spill in 1969 blighted the southern California coastline, while strikes in Britain resulted in power

1. Cyd Charisse
with Gene Kelly
in *Singin' in the
Rain* (1952).

2. Tippi Hedren
as Melanie
Daniels in *The
Birds* (1963).

1. Meghan Markle at the Commonwealth Day Service 2020.

2. Gwyneth Paltrow in *Great Expectations* (1998).

cuts and rubbish piling up in streets. As cities were choked with smog and reports on the dangers of hazardous waste became more and more common, the 1970s were increasingly marked by a rise in environmental awareness. These ecological concerns meant that earthy, natural tones became heavily influential on design aesthetics as people sought to bring the natural world into their lives. We think of avocado green as being everywhere during the 1970s, and not just for the infamous bathroom suite considered a symbol of retro bad taste, but also in fashion design – from Laura Ashley's floral smock dresses to skirts and blouses by Marks and Spencer. In a fashion spread in *Glamour* magazine in November 1972, models wore a range of green sports clothes, such as olive ski overalls, and a forest-green tracksuit and ski jacket. The message was clear – green was about embracing life and the great outdoors.

While the pale, muted green of avocado flesh was for a time considered passé, it underwent a complete image overhaul as the symbol of the millennial hipster. Their love for avocado toast was well and truly documented on Instagram, and in 2020, 6.25 billion avocados were estimated to have been consumed in the United States. The seemingly wholesome fruit, whose farming in fact is embroiled in controversy, was used to demonstrate the frivolity of young people, and in the case of the *Daily Mail*, to blame the Duchess of Sussex, Meghan Markle for fuelling deforestation and human rights abuses through her love of avocados. Maybe as a form of subliminal revenge against her critics, who complained that she was too "woke", Markle wore a glossy green Emilia Wickstead cape dress and matching William Chambers hat to perform one of her last duties as a working senior member of the royal family at the annual Commonwealth Day Service in March 2020.

With the millennial popularity of avocados, and the immediate concern for the environment spearheaded by new movements like Extinction Rebellion, it was no wonder that breezy pistachio and lime shades, along with olive and muted greens, returned to fashion in the 2010s. Instagram was filled with images of interiors with houseplants or kitsch jungle prints, revealing a desire to bring nature indoors to counteract city living and worries about the planet. As consumers became more invested in environmental issues, they sought respite from the stress of political upheaval.

Like the cool of cucumber water and the relaxation of peppermint tea, green was a calming influence and began to dominate the palettes of designers. In the Autumn/Winter 2019/2020 collection, Valentino showcased a green goddess dress with elaborate headdress, and a sequined net gown in the deepest forest green. For Spring 2020, Marc Jacobs wrapped a model in an elaborate green plastic coat, with a hood like that of a flower garland, and a parrot-green suit reminiscent of a 1970s Hitchcock heroine. As singer Billie Eilish championed slime green for her hair and oversized clothing, representing her positive mental health, *Vanity Fair* wrote in August 2019: "Against all odds, clothing, hair dye, and beauty products the colour of slime have remained steadily popular for several years now. 'Toxic green,' they call it. 'Shrek core,' if you prefer, or maybe 'alien chic.'"

Reflective of this revival of green, in 2013 Pantone named "Emerald" their Colour of the Year, and in 2017 it was "Greenery", described as "a fresh and zesty yellow-green shade" that allowed people to "take a deep breath, oxygenate and reinvigorate", adding that "the more submerged people are in modern life, the greater their innate craving to immerse themselves in the physical beauty and inherent unity of the natural world." This is a truth that has been evident for centuries: the colour green, with all its connotations and complexities, finds popularity at times when we collectively need a respite from the repressiveness of our reality, and an escape into a place of nature and beauty.

1. Billie Eilish performing in Miami for her Where Do We Go? world tour.

2. Valentino, haute couture A/W 2019/2020.

Barefoot and swinging a baseball bat, Beyoncé strolls down the street in a ruffled mustard-yellow gown by Roberto Cavalli, taking joy in smashing up cars and shop windows as sweet revenge on her cheating partner. The scene is featured in the music video for 'Hold Up', from 2016's *Lemonade*, and the colour yellow represents her positivity and makes her stand out from the crowd. It was a fashion moment that sparked a comeback for zesty, buttery shades in fashion, as well as adding a tinge of subversion to a colour that is so often linked with happiness.

Yellow

Yellow brings thoughts of optimism and summer days, like sunflowers opening their petals and basking in the sun, or the acid-yellow smiley face printed on posters and T-shirts at 1990s raves. Think of Emma Stone's yellow dress in *La La Land* (2016), eye-popping against the purple and blue of the night sky, the filtered, sunlit images on Instagram or the egg-yolk yellow that Pantone chose to represent Generation Z in 2018.

Yellow, ranging from magnolia, butter and lemon to sunflower, saffron, mustard and fluorescent, is a psychological primary colour that is said to directly correlate with emotions. While it can be stimulating, boosting feelings of optimism, it can also be overwhelming and can have negative connotations. Its long wavelength makes it one of the first colours we see, so it becomes an obvious choice as a visible marker on utilitarian clothing, to ensure those working on roads or on building sites can be seen.

For many cultures, yellow was the colour that represented the sun and gold, two valuable products – one for its life-giving force, the other for its splendour and wealth. For the Romans, yellow was also the colour of honey and bees, and ripe grain. Ceres, the goddess of the harvest and fertility, was often depicted in a yellow dress, with a crown of wheat on her blonde hair.

The colour yellow is used across India to celebrate the Indian New Year and the love festival Gangaur, in tribute to the goddess Gauri, and yellow saris are often worn as an auspicious marker to celebrate the arrival of spring.

Because of its connections to the sun, and to growth and prosperity, yellow is considered dazzling and warm, and just as light cuts through black and destroys the evil of night, yellow represents a positive force.

But because of its visibility, it has also been used for one of the most destructive, hateful symbols in history: the yellow star. Following the outbreak of the Second

World War, the Nazis forced Jews both in Germany and in occupied territories to wear a yellow Star of David on their clothing, which acted as a means of identification and segregation, as a prelude to sending Jews to ghettos and then to concentration camps – changing the connotations of the colour to those of fear and persecution. As Goethe once wrote: "Yellow is a gay, soft, and joyous colour, but in poor light it quickly becomes unpleasant, and the slightest mixing makes it dirty, ugly and uninteresting."

Yellow silk and chrysanthemums

For the 2015 Met Gala, and its theme of "China: Through the Looking Glass", Rihanna chose to wear a yellow silk gown with an enormous 16-foot (4.8-metre) fur-trimmed cape by Chinese designer Guo Pei. The dress, and cape, went viral for its comparison to an omelette, but at its heart, it was a deliberate tribute to the history of China. Guo Pei began her career as a designer at the end of the Cultural Revolution, a period that purged fashion and the arts, and so she chose to allude to her country's rich traditions through the dress. She decorated it with auspicious dragons embroidered in pearls, and silk flowers restored after they were found in a factory abandoned during the Cultural Revolution, while the overwhelming use of yellow was a high-status colour for many centuries.

In 1903, New Orleans painter Katharine Augusta Carl visited the Forbidden City in Beijing to paint the portrait of the Empress Dowager Cixi, who had risen from teenage concubine to the de facto leader of the Qing dynasty from 1861. To shape her image overseas, Cixi invited the American artist to create the portrait, which was displayed at the 1904 World's Fair in St Louis, and then presented to President Theodore Roosevelt. The empress sat regally for her portrait, dressed in a vivid yellow silk gown, which glowed against the dark printed wallpaper and rich mahogany of the mirror that frames her.

In ancient China, yellow was one of the five colours of the Five Element Theory, which was used in philosophy, medicine and feng shui; as it represented the Earth, it was considered the most precious. Yellow was the colour of gold and wealth, the glare of the sun, and the chrysanthemum flower, which was a symbol of longevity and health. It was such a precious colour that during certain eras, only emperors and empresses were allowed to wear it. During the Qing dynasties (1644–1912), yellow was the exclusive colour of the imperial family. As recorded in *Huangchao liqi tushi* (*Illustrations of Imperial Ritual Paraphernalia*), dated from 1760 to 1766, bright yellow could only be worn for the dragon robes and court robes of the emperor and empress, crowned princes could only wear apricot yellow and other princes were only permitted to dress in golden yellow.

The Yellow Emperor, Gongsun Xuanyuan (2711–2598 BCE), the first of five mythical yellow emperors who shaped China as a centralized state, founded the vital aspects of its culture. It was said that his wife Lady Lei-Tzu discovered silk when a cocoon fell from a mulberry tree into her cup of tea, and as she unravelled it, she revealed a clump of silken threads. Silk was one of ancient China's most precious commodities, threaded with secrecy, and legends had been woven around the ancient art of cultivating the *Bombyx mori*, or domestic silk moth, especially when they were silkworms, or larvae. Harvesting the silk from their cocoons was a highly secretive skill known as "sericulture", which other civilizations tried to seek out. By the Shang dynasty (1600–1046 BCE), silk was an important part of religious ceremony and sacrifice, and empresses oversaw their own silkworm farms within the palace walls.

Yellow pigments and dyes
Yellow is one of the most common colours available in nature. While the oldest surviving textile fabric was red,

found in the Indus Valley from around 3000 or 4000 BCE, it's possible that yellow had been used earlier because of the sheer number of plants that can turn fabric yellow.

Pomegranate was used as early as 2000 BCE by the ancient Mesopotamians to create a yellow dye. They also used sumac, derived from the crushed leaves and twigs of the tree, for dyeing leather, which created a yellow-brown tone. Dyer's broom, a shrub found in grassland throughout Europe and North America, is believed to have been used for yellow dye by the Vikings, as well as in England from the ninth to the eleventh centuries. Yellowwood was used in France and Germany from the thirteenth to the nineteenth century.

Before the invention of synthetic dyes, the deepest and most expensive yellow came from hand-picked saffron, which provided rich golden tones that shimmered like a cloth of gold. As one of the most valued and expensive of yellow and orange dyes, the colour, and the spice, is produced from the long, thin stigmas, or enlarged sexual organs, of the saffron crocus.

Saffron was first harvested as a wildflower in ancient Greece, and traces have been found in cave art in Mesopotamia dating back at least 50,000 years, and in wall frescoes at the Minoan Akrotiri settlement on the Greek island of Santorini, which depict women and monkeys picking saffron under the guidance of a goddess.

Archaeologists have uncovered that for the Minoans, saffron was exclusively used by women and girls for perfume, cosmetics and for dyeing their distinctive short yellow jackets. Women were also the primary harvesters, and so the colour derived from saffron was deemed feminine. Ancient Greek priestesses and women of high status wore saffron-dyed robes, including at festivals honouring the earth goddess Demeter and her daughter Persephone. The Romans also embraced saffron as a way to display the wealth of their empire.

1. *Portrait of Madame de Pompadour* (1848), Charles Auguste Steuben.

2. Michelle Williams at the 78th Academy Awards, 2006.

3. Rihanna wears Guo Pei, 2015 Met Gala.

Wild saffron is likely to have been traded by the Phoenicians, and was cultivated in Persia, where they learnt the skills required for this delicate, fickle crop, growing them in long, even rows on raked, arid soil. When coming into bloom in autumn the fields are lit up in a wondrous haze of purple. There is only a short time to pick the stamens, and the process is labour-intensive. They should be plucked in the morning, just after the dew has evaporated, and before the flowers wilt in the sun. Around 40,000 flowers are required to produce half a kilo of saffron, and because of this intensiveness, saffron was, and still is considered, one of the most expensive spices in the world. After arriving in Jerusalem in 1099, the Western Crusaders occupied the Holy Land for a hundred years, where they developed a taste for the local tradition of saffron in cooking and medicine. Because it was forbidden to bring saffron from the region, with the threat of severe punishment from Muslim trading areas, many pilgrims illicitly smuggled saffron corms in rugs or wrapped in fabrics. The story of how saffron came to British shores is steeped in myth – it's believed a pilgrim returning from the Middle East during the reign of Edward III smuggled a crocus bulb under his cap.

The Essex wool-trading town Chepying (Market) Walden, became so famous for its fields of saffron by the 1500s that it was renamed Saffron Walden. Saffron was believed to be an effective cure for the bubonic plague, and with the demand for saffron and the deaths of many farmers at the hands of the Black Death, supplies became strained. Saffron began to be grown in other areas of Europe, including Switzerland, then Germany and France.

Henry VII restricted the Irish from using saffron to dye their clothing, as a means of controlling the population through deprivation. Henry VIII was so protective of his precious saffron supplies that he even banned female courtiers from using it to dye their hair. Due to its scarcity and preciousness, it wasn't long before saffron began to be replaced in popularity by the cheaper weld, or dyer's weed (*Reseda luteola*), which had been used as a bright yellow dye dating back to Roman times. This was later joined by the development of Fustic and Quercitron dyes in the sixteenth and eighteenth centuries, respectively.

When it came to painting in yellow, the pigments most relied upon were extremely noxious. Gallstone yellow was created from crushed ox gallstones, and gamboge was sourced from the sap of Garcinia trees from Cambodia. Gamboge was transported to Britain by the East India Company from 1615, and while it was treasured for its sunshine-yellow hues, it was highly toxic and caused unpleasant side effects for the workers who handled it.

Another yellow pigment, known as Indian yellow, was commonly used by both Indian painters and dyers during the Mughal period for art, to paint houses and to colour textiles. Transported as balls of mustard-coloured powder – which gave off a pungent smell of ammonia – the substance made its way to Europe in the late seventeenth century. While the recipe for the dye was shrouded in secrecy, it was later discovered that it was produced from the yellow urine of cows who were fed only with mango leaves. It was used as a paint up until 1910, including by artist J. M. W. Turner for his shimmering landscapes.

When the French chemist Louis Nicolas Vauquelin discovered chrome yellow in 1797, synthesized from lead chromate, it became a favourite of Vincent van Gogh, who used it for his most famous paintings: for his series of sunflowers, and for the stars and lamplight in *The Starry Night*. But its high lead content led to rumours that it contributed to his madness. Van Gogh wrote to his brother from the south of France in 1888: "The sun dazzles me and goes to my head, a sun, a light that I can only call yellow, sulphur yellow, lemon yellow, golden yellow. How lovely yellow is!"

The negativity of yellow

The golden hues of yellow have not always been considered as valuable as the precious metal they resembled. By the Middle Ages, yellow was tinged with negativity. It came to imply illness, sickness and jaundice, and was linked to yellow bile, one of the four bodily humours. While there were many natural substances that could be used to create yellow fabrics, the colour faded quickly in comparison to long-lasting reds and blues, and with these qualities came a sense of distrust.

In European society, outcasts – those who were deformed, diseased or had committed a crime – were made to wear a yellow scarf, hat or badge, to mark them out. Saffron may have been considered an aphrodisiac in Roman times, but in the fourteenth and fifteenth centuries in Venice, yellow became a marker for prostitutes, who were required to wear yellow scarves at all times. Executioners were commonly depicted in medieval art dressed in yellow. It was a colour that came to depict traitors, and was used to mark the homes of those who had become bankrupt.

Artists in the medieval and Renaissance period began using yellow to show the duplicity of Judas, such as the yellow cape he wears as he embraces Jesus in the fresco *Kiss of Judas* by Giotto di Bondone, on the wall of a chapel in Padua. The yellow of Judas's clothing not only marked him as a traitor, but also signified that he was Jewish.

The enforcement of a yellow badge for Jews was a stigma that dates back to the Middle Ages, where it was a custom that was widespread across Europe at different times following a decree by the Fourth Lateran Council in 1215 that Jews must distinguish themselves from non-Jews. In 1274, for example, King Edward I introduced a law requiring Jews to wear a yellow patch, until ordering their expulsion from England in 1290. Sometimes, as Michel Pastoureau argues in his book about yellow, these patches combined yellow with other colours, including black, white, green and red. Another marker was the yellow pointed hat, or *Judenhut* in German, which appeared in some places across Europe from the twelfth to seventeenth century, and was at times enforced.

The yellow of the two Annes

When Catherine of Aragon died in January 1536, three years after her humiliating divorce from Henry VIII, the king and his second wife Anne Boleyn controversially appeared in the royal court on the day of her funeral wearing matching yellow. The Tudors favoured yellow as the colour of the sun and hope, and Henry VIII chose to wear it for each of his weddings. But it was considered in bad taste to wear yellow after Catherine's death, when others, including Catherine's daughter Mary, wore the traditional black for mourning.

Eric Ives, in *The Life and Death of Anne Boleyn* (2005) writes that they both appeared at court dressed in "joyful yellow" and that they "triumphantly paraded" their daughter Elizabeth to church. In the contemporary account by chronicler Edward Hall, he described how, on the day of the funeral, "Quene Anne ware yelowe for the mournyng." As recorded in *Letters and Papers, Foreign and Domestic, of the Reign of Henry VIII* (1887) Eustace Chapuys, who served as the imperial ambassador to England from 1525 to 1549, reported that on hearing the news, the king exclaimed, "God be praised that we are free from all suspicion of war", and that the following day, "the King was clad all over in yellow, from top to toe, except the white feather he had in his bonnet, and the Little Bastard [Elizabeth I] was conducted to mass with trumpets and other great triumphs. After dinner the King entered the room in which the ladies danced, and there did several things like one transported with joy."

The positive qualities of yellow were also dampened in another infamous event – when Anne Turner was hanged in 1615 for her role in the murder of Sir Thomas Overbury, a courtier to James I. Turner worked as an assistant to society beauty Frances Howard, Countess of Somerset, and also owned a series of houses of "ill repute", where she mixed in London's high and low circles.

She had links to apothecaries that sold precious substances, and with access to saffron, she ran a trade in applying yellow starch to linen ruffs and cuffs, as it became a London fashion for a few years. Turner's downfall came when she assisted Frances Howard and the king's favourite, Robert Carr, in poisoning Overbury because of his disapproval of Carr's affair with Howard. Anne was tried along with her accomplices and was sentenced to death. The judge, Lord Chief Justice Coke, pronounced her "a whore, a bawd, a sorcerer, a witch, a papist, a felon, and a murderer" and ordered her to be hanged in the bright yellow starched ruffs that she brought into vogue "so that the same might end in shame and detestation".

As Alastair Bellany described in his 1995 journal article "Mistress Turner's Deadly Sins", included with her perceived list of sins was "her invention and promotion of the starched yellow ruff", which seemed to represent her aggressive sexuality. Sir Simonds d'Ewes, writing in the 1630s, wrote that Turner "had first brought up that vain and foolish use of yellow starch, coming herself to her trial in a yellow band and cuffs", and that on the day of her execution, the hangman "had his band and his cuffs of the same colour" as a way of further deterring the fashion. Her case was one of the most sensational of the seventeenth century, and she became known as The Poisoner with the Yellow Ruff. With her notoriety, saffron-coloured ruffs quickly fell out of favour.

Yellow continued to be considered in a bad light centuries later. During the second half of the nineteenth century, French novels that were considered too risqué and controversial were often bound in yellow covers, which both branded them as illicit and marketed them as a signifier of decadence when they were sold cheaply at transport hubs. It was later a term attached to a sensational form of journalism in the United States. In China, yellow implies pornography, and a genre of Italian horror movie is known as *giallo*, meaning "yellow".

All that glitters

In medieval times, gold was the only truly acceptable form of yellow, given the negative connotations of yellow. Gold was considered spiritually divine, and much sought-after in trade along the Silk Road. From when it was first mined over 7,000 years ago and burnished into jewellery and ornaments, gold was valued for its rarity and expense. Alexander the Great was believed to be particularly fond of cloth woven with gold. He advanced through Persia around 331 BCE with his army of "Immortals", who were described by the Latin writer Justin as wearing golden collars or "cloth variegated with gold".

As silk travelled along the Silk Road from China to Persia and the Mediterranean, it became a prized fabric for Roman citizens. While Tyrian purple silk was the most coveted of colours, the tyrannical Emperor Commodus (161–192 CE) possessed a garment with stripes of bright yellow silk that was said to be so beautiful, it appeared to have been threaded with gold.

Cloth of gold was one of the most sought-after fabrics for European kings and queens in the medieval ages, where silk was interwoven with fine golden threads to create a splendid, sumptuous glimmer. It was particularly popular in the era of the Tudors. A portrait of Arthur, Prince of Wales, from around 1500 depicts him wearing a gown of cloth of gold, with a sable and velvet doublet, to create an impressively wealthy image. Henry VIII, his brother, spared no expense when it came to his own wardrobe and introduced a sumptuary law to dictate that cloth of gold could only be worn by royalty, and it was lavishly used for the coronation gowns of Mary I and Elizabeth I, as well as for royal wedding gowns. In 1520, Europe's two extravagant young rulers, King Henry VIII and Francis I of France, came face to face at a grand encounter known as the Field of the Cloth of Gold, as they dressed in their finest, and most expensive, gold cloth, to outdo one another in their displays of power.

The glimmer of gold was displayed in all its sumptuous glory in Gustav Klimt's 1907 portrait of Adele Bloch-Bauer, a wealthy Viennese socialite who was his patron and friend. In creating her gold dress that blends in with the background, Klimt was inspired by the Byzantine mosaics of the Empress Theodora, who wore brilliant gold to enhance her image as a divine being. It was the last of Klimt's works in his golden phase, and he used gold leaf to paint her dress and the background. In 1941, the painting was seized from the home of the Jewish Bloch-Bauers by the Nazis, and in 2000, Adele Bloch-Bauer's niece, Maria Altmann, took Austria to court to return the work to her family, as depicted in the 2015 film *Woman in Gold* starring Helen Mirren.

Nowadays, gold can be considered tacky and "dictator chic" if worn excessively, but gold dresses are particularly popular on the red carpet, with *Elle* magazine describing the gold dress as "the little black dress' sexy younger sister. She's vivacious, hypnotic and utterly unstoppable." Marilyn Monroe was famously sewn into a golden pleated gown designed by Travilla, which was far too risqué to be shown in full in *Gentlemen Prefer Blondes* (1953), and Farrah Fawcett matched the Oscars statue she was handing out while presenting at the 1978 Academy Awards. At the 2018 Met Gala, Kim Kardashian displayed her love of ultra-glamour in a skin-tight, gold Versace gown, with cross embellishments reminiscent of Byzantine relics, summing up the gaudy glory of Donatella Versace's designs.

1. Natalie Wood in *Sex and the Single Girl* (1964).

2. Kim Kardashian wearing gold Versace for the 2018 Met Gala.

3. Kate Moss in New York, 2003.

The yellow dress

Despite the negative history around yellow, it was given an image makeover in the eighteenth century following the French court fashion for light, bright silks, and a trend towards chinoiserie, which embraced the imperial yellow of China in textiles and decorative arts. A canary-yellow gown from 1760 is in the collection of the Metropolitan Museum of Art, and was designed in the *robe à la Française* style. Yellow is the first colour the human eye notices, and a gown of this colour was designed to ensure that all eyes were drawn to the dress – and the wearer – when making a dramatic entrance. An 1848 portrait of Madame de Pompadour by Charles Auguste Steuben, depicts her in a brilliant yellow gown; romanticizing yellow as the fashionable colour of the time.

In July 2020, *Nylon* magazine stated that the yellow dress was just as iconic in film and pop culture as the red dress. From Natalie Wood's yellow gown by Edith Head in *Sex and the Single Girl* (1964) to Kate Hudson in *How to Lose a Guy in 10 Days* (2003), a yellow dress was used to signify a moment of love or happiness. Throughout the romantic comedy *Sex and the Single Girl*, Edith Head kept to a black and white palette for Wood, to suit her character: a psychologist who doesn't stray from her convictions in offering advice for single women. It's only in the final scene that she embraces colour – a canary-yellow dress with matching scarf, worn when she finally accepts she's fallen in love with Tony Curtis's character.

Similarly, Kate Hudson's advice columnist Andie, in *How to Lose a Guy in 10 Days*, is singularly confident in the dating advice she gives to her readers, on the surefire ways to ensure you get dumped by a man. The yellow dress, designed by Carolina Herrera in consultation with the film's costume designer Karen Patch, was chosen for the pinnacle of the movie, when her unwitting rival, Matthew McConaughey, realizes he's fallen in love with her. With a back that plunges to the base of the spine, the shimmering silk gown was chosen for wearing to an upscale PR event for a diamond brand, where she is the standout woman in the room. It was particularly memorable for being so unusually yellow, and helped to shape the idea of Andie as a trendsetter, choosing the back as her erogenous zone and yellow as her signature colour.

On the red carpet, yellow was a fairly uncommon colour until Michelle Williams's buttercup gown by Vera Wang at the 2006 Academy Awards. Another impactful yellow dress was worn by Kate Moss in 2003 at a magazine party in New York. Moss had picked up the lemon-sherbet chiffon dress from a vintage store in Beverly Hills, and with one shoulder strap coolly hanging down her arm, it was so popular that she recreated it for her one of her sell-out Topshop collaborations, first launched in 2007.

Because yellow isn't as common a colour as red or black, it's unexpected and surprising when it makes an appearance. Costume designer Mary Zophres described yellow as traditionally a "stay away from" colour, until she found the right yellow for her dress, hand-painted with a Matisse-inspired floral print, for *La La Land* (2016). Zophres was inspired by a real-life red carpet appearance of Emma Stone in 2014, where she wore a cap-sleeve canary-yellow dress. The yellow was perfect for representing an ecstatic moment, in which the colour acted as a transition throughout the leading couple's romance and complemented the primary palette of green and blue. With the movement of the skirt, the colour pops against the starlit violet sky as she dances above Los Angeles with Ryan Gosling. Used for the film posters, that scene, and that dress, became an instantly iconic moment.

In the teen movie *Clueless* (1995), Alicia Silverstone defined a new kind of fashion-savvy teenager, twisting on the trend for grunge with her yellow plaid suit. It was designed by Mona May, who wanted her to wear a "cool

1. Stacey Dash and Alicia Silverstone in *Clueless* (1995).

2. Uma Thurman as The Bride in Quentin Tarantino's *Kill Bill: Volume 1* (2003).

3. Emma Stone and Ryan Gosling in *La La Land* (2016).

yellow" to go with her blonde hair. "Cher is glowing when you first meet her. The color has energy," said Mona May. "It was the first day at school, so we always wanted to make sure she pops." She added: "Yellow is very powerful, but still, to me, more of an innocent color," suiting Cher's role as the most popular girl at school, yet not the typical high-school "mean girl". While pink became the pervading colour of teenage girls in the 2000s, for the 1990s, yellow was the funky, bright and optimistic tint that defied expectation.

The yellow siren

The bold cartoon-colour visuals of Quentin Tarantino's *Kill Bill Volume 1* (2003) have become a fixture of popular culture, particularly the dominant yellow that blares out throughout the film. It's the colour of the car dubbed the Pussy Wagon, and of the costume worn by Uma Thurman as the vengeful Bride. It's become one of the most identifiable movie costumes, going beyond its original homage to Bruce Lee in *Game of Death* (1978).

"I've never done a movie before where I took a colour and made it the colour of the film," said Quentin Tarantino. "Here it was yellow, and I was jumping off Uma's blonde hair. I wanted blonde to be the colour of the movie, as opposed to my other movies, which are more aural. But this is the visual equivalent of my aural, everything coming of her blondeness."

Uma Thurman's yellow and black striped tracksuit gives her the appearance of an angry hornet, acting as a warning sign, just as the contrasting colours are used in nature by insects like wasps and bees to offer a caution to predators. The film's costume designer Catherine Marie Thomas said: "Uma's yellow tracksuit is pivotal. She's a trained assassin in a revenge film and her wardrobe reflects that. She's not hiding from anybody."

While Bruce Lee's tracksuit was a one-piece jumpsuit, a two-piece was chosen to be more flattering. Fifty copies were made for Thurman and her stunt doubles to allow for blood stains and damage as she leaps, kicks and flies through the air. There's also a matching motorbike outfit and helmet, worn for speeding through the neon streets of Tokyo.

Kill Bill inspired the visuals of Lady Gaga's extended music video, *Telephone* (2010), which not only borrowed the primary colours of the film, but adapted the yellow and black of Thurman's tracksuit into a costume made of crime-scene tape. The concept of the music video, Lady Gaga said, was to take "the idea that America is full of young people that are inundated with information and technology and turn it into something that was more of a commentary on the kind of country that we are." In prison, as she's stripped of her clothes, removing the trappings of her persona, she's left vulnerable, and almost naked, in her cell. It was a commentary on the negative nature of fame, and how her body is publicly disseminated.

"The crime scene tape was one of the images that we had in mind," director Jonas Åkerlund said. "We improvised it and it ended up becoming one of her outfits and it looked really cool. It was supposed to be about being claustrophobic in her cell."

The yellow vest

The high-visibility vest became a symbol of protest in France, as part of the *gilets jaunes* movement that began with motorists in rural France who were protesting against fuel tax. Because of a pre-existing law in France that all motorists must carry a yellow vest in their cars, it became a symbol not only of government control placed on motorists, but also of the working man and the urgency of their protest, as the vest's purpose is to be used as a distress sign. It is also an inexpensive, convenient and immediately recognizable way to show unity as part of mass movement. The *New York Times* called it "one of the most effective protest garments in history", and the power of the yellow vest meant it spread to other countries, where it was used to signify many different movements, including pro-Brexit protesters in the UK, an anti-Islamic group in Australia and anti-immigration protesters in Finland. It not only identifies the wearer as part of a protest, but also identifies those who are not – with stories of people donning a yellow vest in order to feel safe when passing through crowds of protestors. In Paris in 2019, there was a counterdemonstration of red scarves, again using a simple item as a call to arms. But this immediately created a connotation of the bourgeoisie, as a red scarf is worn for style, while a yellow vest is a practical item.

For some, the yellow vest is a social movement for the people, a class signifier to show allegiance for the working class in the face of the government. For others, it is a rallying cry for the far right, which demonstrates how an everyday piece of clothing can have countless meanings attached to it depending on the situation.

Fast-food fashion and Gen-Z yellow

Yellow was a representation of harmony during the counterculture of the 1960s, with the call sign to come to San Francisco and "wear some flowers in your hair". The Beatles' *Yellow Submarine* album and movie spoke of love and peace, and Donovan's song "Mellow Yellow", about being "cool and laid-back", was an expression derived from James Joyce's book *Ulysses* (1920). The character Leopold Bloom describes his wife Molly Bloom, and how "I do indeed explore the plump mellow yellow smellow melons of her rump".

Just as yellow represented the hopefulness of the love fests of the 1960s, it made a return for the second summer of love in 1988. The acid-yellow smiley face was once again a beacon of hedonism that spoke for a generation of young people who discovered themselves, and a new joy, at raves, under the effects of ecstasy. It was, as singer-songwriter Shaun Ryder remembered, "When life suddenly went from black and white to Technicolor."

The smiley face had originally been designed in 1963 by American advertiser Harvey Ball for an insurance company to motivate their workers, and it then appeared on stickers at free festivals during the psychedelic movement. But it took on a whole new meaning as the face of acid house after being adopted for the original London acid-house club night, Shoom, in 1988, followed by use on album covers, badges and flyers, and in fashion design.

The *Sun* newspaper had been on board with the acid house scene at first, describing it as "cool and groovy" and offering smiley T-shirts for sale. But a few weeks later, it changed tack to warn of the dangers. Acid house was now, according to the newspaper, a "hellish nightmare engulfing thousands of youngsters". Topshop even banned the sale of smiley T-shirts on the back of this sort of negative press.

The smiley face took on a wider meaning as one of the most popular emojis for virtual communication, but as millennials looked back with nostalgia at the early 1990s, the acid-yellow circle made a comeback in fashion as a symbol of rave culture. For his Spring 2015 menswear collection, Jeremy Scott, head designer at Moschino, brought back the smiley face, for a bright yellow patent jacket with the black lines of the smile on the back. The year before, Scott had become a social media phenomenon when he fully embraced the kitsch yellow of chocolate-bar wrappers, SpongeBob SquarePants, and fast food for his debut Autumn 2014 ready-to-wear collection for Moschino.

With the notion of yellow appealing to the feel-good emotions in children, which will encourage parents to buy, yellow is the colour of the fast food industry. McDonald's red and yellow colour scheme is the most recognizable in the world, chosen as a stimulating combination that offers comfort and happiness from the yellow, and excitement and hunger from the red. Scott embraced trash culture and junk food with his bright and brash designs featuring the label's heart design reconfigured as McDonald's golden arches, with slim-fit jackets and skirts in bold yellow and red. The kitsch aesthetics of fast food, with their often-yellow wrappers and logos, appealed to modern consumers, and fitted with an embracing of yellow as a fun, fleeting colour for instant gratification.

Pantone introduced "Gen Z yellow" in 2018, but the name was coined by *Repeller* writer Haley Nahman in 2017 when she noticed a shift from millennial pink to yellow across her Instagram feed. It offered a new hope for the future, an energetic colour to reinvigorate at a time when concerns around politics and the environment could feel overwhelming.

Nahman said she first noticed the trend with artist Petra Collins using yellow lights in her shoots, rather than the pink she'd become known for, including in Selena Gomez's 'Fetish' music video, where she was dressed in lemon yellow and filmed in a hazy, filtered sunshine, as she smashes up her kitchen. The video was credited with sparking a trend for a fresh yellow aesthetic in music videos.

"Gen-Z Yellow is the natural evolution of millennial pink," wrote Nahman. "It maintains that pleasing-to-the-eye softness of the sweetest shades of millennial pink, but without the over-played infantilization. It's both nostalgic *and* modern. It has zest, energy, optimism."

While pink is soft and pretty, yellow is energetic. It may not always have been perceived in a positive light, but it can still evoke happiness and warmth, making it the perfect colour for a summer's day, and the promise of a bright future.

1. Audrey Hepburn in *Charade* (1963), wearing a coat by Givenchy.

2. Street style at Seoul Fashion Week, October 2019.

3. Roberto Cavalli's A/W 2016/2017 gown, worn by Beyoncé in her 'Hold Up' video.

4. Moschino, menswear S/S 2015, the London Collections.

5. Valentino, haute couture S/S 2010.

As Halle Berry emerged from the sea in an orange bikini as Bond girl Jinx in 2002's *Die Another Day*, she brought the often maligned colour back into the spotlight. Her bikini, by the brand Eres, with its custom-made knife belt, was a tribute to Ursula Andress as Honey Ryder in the first Bond film, *Dr. No* (1962), and with images of Berry splashed across newspapers and magazines as publicity, it reaffirmed orange's place as the hue you can't look away from. It's also a colour of love, represented by the fruit in Sandro Botticelli's *Primavera* (c. 1470) and *The Birth of Venus* (c. 1485–86), and by the actress known as the Love Goddess, auburn-haired Rita Hayworth.

Orange

Orange has a reputation for being difficult to pull off, with fashion magazines in the Victorian era warning women to be careful of the colour, as it was unflattering to certain complexions. In the West it's considered a "marmite" hue – some love it, some hate it – but it's also the colour that is completely entwined with a season. Veering from warm gold to amber to burnt sienna, it's reminiscent of the different shades of autumn, of carved pumpkin lanterns at Halloween, the scent of spiced pumpkin pie in the air and burnished leaves crunching on the ground.

As a combination of red and yellow, orange conveys heat and energy, evocative of the warm embers of a fire or the glow of a sunset. It is also tinged with a mouth-watering succulence as the hue of the juiciest of citrus fruits, conjuring up thoughts of mangoes, apricots, clementines and tangerines, and of drinking chilled glasses of Aperol Spritz in the summer. This symbolism is apt because of the often-asked question of which came first – the colour or the fruit. Derived from the Persian *narang*, for the fruit and tree, "orange" is one of the newest colour names in the English language, the first recorded use being in 1512. Orange was linked to Protestantism in Europe through the Dutch King William of Orange (1650–1702). His name may have derived from a French town called Aurenja, but either way, it came to be entwined with the colour. As a result, orange has a long-lasting legacy in the Netherlands, where it represents the Orange-Nassau royal family, and decorates the country's flag and the uniform of their football teams.

Because of its sunny disposition, orange often makes a fashion comeback during periods of optimism, such as the roaring 1920s and the youthquake of the 1960s, when orange was promoted as the way to brighten up a wardrobe. With its energy and intensity, it often veers into bad taste because it clashes with other shades, becoming murky when mixed with greens and browns, as was the fashion in the 1970s.

Orange is considered overpowering when worn on its own, often being used to warn of danger. It's the colour of Guantanamo Bay jumpsuits, the chemical Agent Orange, traffic signals and road warnings. Tori Amos sang of "the power of orange knickers under my petticoat" – the feeling of empowerment that comes from wearing something bright and shocking that's concealed from view. Once orange is unleashed, it's difficult to look away from.

From the fruit to the colour
Although a rusty ochre pigment, made from fine clay and iron oxide, may have been used for prehistoric cave paintings, and ancient Egyptians painted tombs with realgar, a toxic mineral pigment, orange is the most recent of the colours of the rainbow to be officially named. The English word for the tangy colour came after the sweet fruit first arrived from the Middle East in the sixteenth century.

To describe something as orange-coloured in Old-English, spoken between the fifth and twelfth centuries, was to refer to it as *geoluread*, meaning "yellow-red". In Geoffrey Chaucer's *The Nun's Priest's Tale* (c. 1390s), a fox that enters into a barnyard is described as having a colour "betwixe yelow and reed". The robin's red breast and the red fox are in fact orange, but when there wasn't a name for that particular tone, the closest match, "red", was used in its place.

The perfectly round citrus fruit is believed to have been cultivated in China around 4,500 years, and then transported west via the Silk Road trade routes through India and Persia. Early in the fifteenth century, Portuguese traders brought sweet oranges from India to Europe, with the first written reference, a bill of sale from an Italian trader for 15,000 sweet oranges, dating from 1472. When Europeans first cast their eyes on the fruit, they found they lacked a word for it, initially referring to oranges as "golden apples", and naming the colour "tawny" or "quince".

1. Halle Berry as Jinx in *Die Another Day* (2002).

2. Rita Hayworth performing 'The Heat is On' in *Miss Sadie Thompson* (1953).

The Sanskrit word for orange tree, *nāraṅga*, is believed to have derived from the older Dravidian word *naru*, meaning "fragrant". It became the root of the word as it travelled from east to west, becoming *naranga* in India, *naranj* in Arabic and *naranja* in Spanish, before evolving to "an orange" in English. Another route taken was from the Italian word for the fruit, *melarancio*, from which came the Old French *orenge*.

By the sixteenth century, the sweet orange was introduced as a luxury product, cultivated in elaborate and expensive greenhouses known as *orangeries*, and making appearances in market stalls, with the orange tree as a status symbol in the homes of influential Europeans like the De Medici family in Florence. Believed to help in warding off illness and the plague, oranges were studded with cloves to make pomanders, which hung from the waist or were worn around the neck as a popular accessory for the Tudors. Nell Gwyn, the mistress of Charles II, was one of the scantily clad and flirtatious "orange girls" of the Restoration era, selling imported oranges to audiences in London theatres.

According to Kassia St Clair, orange was first recorded in relation to clothes in 1502, when records showed that Elizabeth of York bought "slevys of orange colour sarsenet" for Margaret Tudor. In a 1544 portrait by Master John, Mary Tudor, eldest daughter of King Henry VIII, is depicted wearing a luxurious gown with a brilliant orange bodice and red and white sleeves, suiting her reputation as a fashion-lover who sourced the finest Italian textiles, before she became a devout queen.

Gradually, "orange" began to enter into literary works, with a reference in *A Midsummer Night's Dream* (c. 1596), in which William Shakespeare described one of Bottom's stage beards as being "orange tawny", using it as a descriptor to brighten up brown tones. In 1576, an English translation of a third-century military history written in

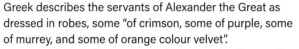

Greek describes the servants of Alexander the Great as dressed in robes, some "of crimson, some of purple, some of murrey, and some of orange colour velvet".

It wasn't until the seventeenth century that "orange" was widespread as a term for the colour, with its frequency aided by Isaac Newton's discovery of the light spectrum in 1672. When he shone sunlight through a glass prism and carried out a series of analysis, he built on the six basic colours – black, white, red, green, blue and yellow – by removing black and white as colours, and elevating orange into the colour spectrum, alongside violet, indigo, blue, green, yellow and red.

Dyeing textiles with orange

There may have been no word for the colour orange until the sixteenth century, but it was described in historical dye books with a variety of words. In the *Stockholm Papyrus* (300–400 CE), it was likely referred to as "darker yellow" and "gold colour"; and in the *Segreti per Colori*, from the mid fifteenth century, it was described as "saffron coloured".

Orange could be achieved by dipping a fabric first in a vat of red dye, and then in yellow, or by combining the two dye baths together. There were also other dyestuffs used to create these warm shades. Madder root, widely used for red fabrics, could produce orange tones with an acid mordant. Onion skin, traditionally a yellow dye, could also be used for orange when combined with an alum mordant. One of the most prolific dye manuals, *The Plictho of Gioanventura Rosetti*, first published in 1548, included recipes for making an orange dye with fustet, a dyestuff from the European smoke tree, when combined with alum. The manual also described a recipe for creating a "quince" shade: "To mordant, 20 pounds of alum and 2 pounds of grain [kermes]. Then take 8 pounds of weld and if you can't find weld take 'quilitia' or sweet wood, or 'cioretta' and to this herb there should be 15 pounds of fustet."

ANNO · DNI   1 5 4 4

LADI MARI   DOVGHTER TO
THE MOST   VERTVOVS PRINCE
KINGE HENRI   THE EIGHT

THE AGE OF   XXVIII YERES

1. Portrait of Mary Tudor, 1544

2. George Barbier's illustration of Jeanne Paquin's designs (1912).

As dyers tweaked their recipes for orange, the colour became one of the most popular among the elite classes in Europe. Sumatran and Malaysian brazilwood was imported into Venice in the fifteenth century when it was discovered it could yield a range of reddish tones, from orange to pink to violet, depending on how it was prepared. It began to appear in dyers' manuals for creating a range of red dyes, as well as for achieving orange shades when aided with the use of acid mordants like vinegar and urine.

Rosetti included a recipe using Sumatran brazilwood which would dye wool an orange "loaded with color". His instructions included the use of "20 pounds of alum and three pounds of grain [kermes]", and then "4 pounds of madder of medium-sized lumps in a new bath with ten pails of strong water. Then one must madder it in a new bath. If you can have it of brazil take it if it has not been mastered. Then it needs 70 pounds of fustet and make it come out twice."

In 1662, when Portuguese explorers sailing the South American coastline found trees with orange-red heartwood growing in abundance, they identified them as relatives of the Asian brazilwood. They gave these trees the same name, "brazilwood", and then the region *terra de brasil*, after the word *brasil*, meaning "glowing like a fire". With the exploitation of slave labour in South America to harvest the wood, brazilwood became cheaper to import into Europe, and its wide desirability as a dye coincided with an uptake of the use of "orange" to describe the flame-coloured textiles it produced.

The pulp of the seeds of the *Bixa orellana*, or roucou tree, from central and South America, was also a popular dye for orange fabrics, with the crushed-up seeds providing a pigment called *annatto*, which was utilized as a body paint by the indigenous people. In the 1860 book *600 Miscellaneous Valuable Receipts worth their weight in gold*, published in Pennsylvania, *annotto* was listed as an ingredient, along with pearl ash (an alkaline salt) and alum, for dyeing silk orange.

As explored in the chapter on yellow, saffron had an illustrious history as a fragrant spice and as a dye for feminine yellow robes in ancient Greece and Rome. When saffron reached India, its vibrant colour was considered representative of fire, of the light burning away darkness. As it became a significant part of religious ceremonies, with Hindu priests using it to dye their robes, saffron became a sacred colour representing wisdom and knowledge.

Saffron robes were also traditionally worn by Buddhist monks in India, and as the religion was exported through the East, the colour orange remained a symbol of their modesty and simplicity. While saffron was prohibitively expensive, the earliest monks in Thailand used the readily available heartwood of the jackfruit tree to dye the fabric of their robes orange. The colour of robes was also adopted by the Hare Krishna movement, founded in 1966 in the United States, as a reference to the traditions of Hinduism, on which its core beliefs were based.

In the twentieth century, when India gained independence, the gold-orange of saffron was chosen as one of the colours of the flag, to indicate its importance within India's different religions. The country pulsates with the colour in the vibrant mounds of saffron, ochre, cinnamon and turmeric piled up in market stalls across the country, and in the strings of marigold flowers, used lavishly during festivals and celebrations.

Orange as a symbol of love

As well as being a symbol of wealth, the bountiful orange tree, with its succulent fruit and waxy green leaves, was considered a representation of love and fertility. Botticelli draped the goddess of love, Venus, in orange fabrics in both *Primavera* and *The Birth of Venus*, and featured lush orange groves in the background. Oranges were considered beautiful and romantic, with Giovanni Battista Ferrarius writing in his book about citrus fruit, *Hesperides Sive de Malorum Aureorum Cultura et Usu* (1646): "So I bestow upon this little rounded fruit the merited name of an ornament of the world, for in its golden dress it seems a decoration for the earth."

In addition to being used as a textile dye, saffron was also employed as an orange pigment, and to stabilize green copper pigments, for the prevalent Indian miniature paintings of the Mughal Empire from the sixteenth century, which often depicted love scenes in fertile gardens. In an illustration from 1709, entitled *Bangali Ragini: Folio from a ragamala series (Garland of Musical Modes),* which is part of the collection of the Metropolitan Museum, women in a tropical garden are depicted wearing orange-coloured saris. The illustration was accompanied by a section of a poem in which a woman's sari, "soaked with kesara [saffron], is enchanting". Another work, *Radha and Krishna Walk in a Flowering Grove* (1720), is a paradisiacal tableau, where Radha wears a saffron-coloured sari as she gazes into Krishna's eyes, with the orange of the sun glowing behind them.

In the mid eighteenth century, when lighter, brighter and bold colours became fashionable in Europe, orange replaced red as a desirable colour for furnishings and for fashion. In the Georgian era, orange was a particular favourite for women, and we see it worn in a number of portraits. Nicolas Fouché, in his 1700 portrait *Pomona,* depicted the Roman goddess of fruit trees swathed in an orange tunic, holding peaches in her hand. Jean Ranc similarly depicted Pomona in an orange French-style gown with a basket of fruit, in his painting *Vertumnus and Pomona* (c. 1710–1720).

Pomona was a popular subject of the Pre-Raphaelite painters like Dante Gabriel Rossetti and Edward Burne-Jones in the late nineteenth century, who celebrated nature and Renaissance art with flame-haired heroines dressed in flowing orange or green gowns, surrounded by the lush, verdant hues of nature and trees dotted with orange fruit. English painter Albert Joseph Moore depicted classical decadence with his paintings of women wrapped in peach and orange togas in the paintings *Pomegranates* (1866) and *Midsummer* (1887).

Orange continued to be considered a symbol of love in the twentieth century. By anglicizing her name and dyeing her hair a vibrant auburn, actress Rita Hayworth was transformed from a dark-haired Spanish-American dancer named Margarita Cansino into the all-American "Love Goddess", as she was dubbed. From her breakout role in *Blood and Sand* (1941), for which she was dressed in warm colours to suit her passionate character, Hayworth was often described as "sizzling" on screen, and she was frequently billed as a lustrous redhead. Some editions of posters for her movies, including *Cover Girl* (1944), *Gilda* (1946) and *The Lady from Shanghai* (1947), used orange as a backdrop to reflect her fiery sex-symbol status, which was quite different from her reserved off-screen persona.

Her costumes, sometimes in flame-inspired colours, reflected the passions of the characters she played, and suited her Latin-dancer background, such as a spicy orange Spanish-style skirt in *The Loves of Carmen* (1948). In *Miss Sadie Thompson* (1953), she wears a shimmering, burnished orange dress as she performs the frenetic musical number 'The Heat is On', which takes place in a sweaty South Pacific bar.

She wears another orange gown in 1957's *Pal Joey*, for the scene in the dive bar where Frank Sinatra's Joey sings 'The Lady is a Tramp' to her character, Vera Prentice-Simpson. As a former stripper who is now a wealthy socialite, her saffron strapless silk gown, worn with an orange fur wrap, not only makes her stand out in the gloomy nightclub, but also hints at her past life as a burlesque star. And it shows she's in control as Joey offers himself up to her in the hopes she'll fund his dream nightclub. When she performs 'Bewitched, Bothered and Bewildered', she further embodies the Love Goddess persona in a marigold negligee, with her red hair loose around her shoulders – reminiscent of the famous 1941 *Life* magazine photo that made her the number one pin-up in America.

The clash and complements of orange

When French scientist Nicolas Louis Vauquelin discovered the mineral crocolite in 1797, it led to the 1809 synthesizing of the artificial pigment known as chrome orange. Other synthetics, including cobalt orange, soon followed. Despite the push for brilliantly hued gowns in the Victorian era, and the Pre-Raphaelites and the Impressionists using the colour in their popular paintings, orange was considered too overpowering for most complexions and hair colours.

French chemist Michel Eugène Chevreul, in his book *The Laws of Contrast of Colour* (1857), set out guidelines on how colours should be worn and combined together, hoping that dressmakers would learn from his rules, which took into account the colour of fabrics next to certain skin tones and hair colours. Chevreul said: "Orange is too bright to be elegant. It makes fair complexions blue, whitens those which have an orange tint and gives a green hue to those of a yellow tint."

An 1855 edition of *Godey's Lady's Book* noted: "Orange suits nobody. It whitens a brunette, but that is scarcely a desirable effect, and it is ugly." Similarly, in their 1870 book *Colour in Dress*, authors William and George Audsley advised that orange is "particularly to be avoided by the Fair Blonde". They added that it may "be said to suit Brunettes with more or less positive orange in their complexions, is too brilliant and gaudy to be used in dress, save in very small proportions".

Their view on orange was that it was "a warm, prominent color", and both in nature and art appears to the best advantage when in small quantities, and associated with its contrasting colors, blue and purple" and "is most suitable for winter or very early spring".

While orange was generally rejected as a standalone colour in fashion periodicals, it was considered agreeable when combined with blue, which the Audsleys described as "a perfect harmony". In the summer months, white cotton dresses were often trimmed with orange ribbons, or orange silk gowns were embroidered with white thread. For autumn, sometimes orange was combined with greens and browns to conjure up a seasonal mood.

In the first decades of the twentieth century, the art of fashion illustration boomed, and it was here that the colour orange came into its own. Leading Paris designers like Paul Poiret and Jeanne Paquin commissioned artists to capture his jewel-coloured, Eastern-inspired confections, which he promoted as pieces of art in their own right.

In 1908, French illustrator Paul Iribe introduced the *pochoir* method of stencil printing, based on a Japanese technique, where he applied layers of orange, green and blue pigment to bring to life a romanticized version of Poiret's fashions. Georges Lepape created a series of illustrations of Poiret's designs in 1911, which he bordered with eye-catching orange, depicting art nouveau heroines in citrus-coloured turbans and harem-pant tunics. For the cover of *Les Modes Parisiennes* in April 1912, George Barbier illustrated two models in a moonlit rose garden, with one dressed in an orange lampshade tunic and turban by Paquin, reminiscent of the Mughal miniatures from centuries before. Throughout the 1910s and 1920s, orange was prominent on the art deco cover of *Vogue*, as artists like Lepape used it to bring the era's frivolous fashions to life.

Italian designer Elsa Schiaparelli arrived back in Paris in 1922 as a single mother, having been left by her husband

1. *Vogue* magazine cover, April 1917.

2. Schiaparelli S/S 2017, Paris.

in New York, but set out to use her social and familial connections to be accepted into Parisian society. When she received an invitation for an eminent ball, she went to Galeries Lafayette to purchase four yards of dark blue crêpe de Chine and two yards of orange silk. Inspired by her mentor Paul Poiret, she draped the blue fabric around her body and between her legs, rather than sewing them together, and used the orange silk both for a wide sash around her waist, and wrapped around her head as a turban. She described the reaction when she arrived at the ball as a "small sensation. Nobody had seen anything like it, especially anybody dressed in such a queer way." It was a moment that showed her potential to create showstopping creations, and encouraged her to develop her career as a fashion designer.

One of Schiaparelli's most infamous designs was the lobster dress, created in collaboration with Salvador Dalí in 1937. The lobster design was a favourite motif of the Spanish surrealist artist, who had featured it in his works from 1934, including *New York Dream – Man Finds Lobster in Place of Phone*, and his 1936 lobster telephone sculpture. Dalí drew the initial orange lobster motif for the dress, and Schiaparelli then commissioned silk designer Sache to print it onto a white silk organza dress.

The dress was considered quite risqué in its placing of the vivid lobster on pure white, with the animal's tail covering the body in a sexually suggestive way. It became notorious when the much maligned Wallis Simpson chose it as part of her trousseau for her marriage to Edward VIII, later the Duke of Windsor. Just before the wedding, Cecil Beaton photographed her wearing the dress in the gardens of the Château de Condé, and the images were splashed in an eight-page feature in *Vogue* in May 1937. Simpson had been the primary reason for Edward's abdication in 1936, and the dress, with its splash of orange, further cemented her as a brazen, immoral woman.

As well as being chosen to represent a fiery nature, orange tones were considered particularly ideal for autumn fashions. British *Vogue*, in August 1955, heralded "marigold" as "Sure fire for autumn ... a brand-new, clear palette of colours starting from the palest, budding marigold, blossoming through the tawny shades to a blaze of deep sun-burnt orange". The following month they named "marigold" as one of the significant colours for the autumn, along with "black-browns (the best, a rich coffee-bean colour)".

In March 1960, *Vogue* described the trend for "Hot Orange", noting: "The big excitement in Paris was the terrific use of colour – blazing, primitive colour, both for day and for evening."

From mod minidresses by Pierre Cardin for his mid 1960s space-inspired collection to the flowing Pucci prints that brought together clashing psychedelic colours, orange (and its sister shade, tangerine) was in tune with all the fashion moods of the late 1960s and 1970s. It was a colour for confident young women in Mary Quant and André Courrèges, who weren't afraid to stand out in their orange micro minidresses or vinyl coats, often paired with white go-go boots.

Just as purple featured in the art nouveau style posters of the Haight-Ashbury district of San Francisco, orange was its complementary colour and they competed in vibrant, clashing swirls that captured the acid-tinged mood of the hippie movement. While purple inspired Jimi Hendrix and the band Deep Purple, orange's influence was evident in the name of the electronic band Tangerine Dream, and Led Zeppelin's folk-rock song 'Tangerine' (1970).

By the 1970s, at a time of angst over strikes in Britain and fatigue over the Vietnam War, the dreamy psychedelia of the 1960s became tired, and fashions returned to a more sober conservatism. Orange is a colour that can straddle moods, from bright and cheerful

1. André Courrèges, Winter 1969/1970.

2. Hermès, ready-to-wear S/S 2013, Paris.

3. Michael J Fox as Marty McFly in Back to the Future (1985).

4. Calvin Klein, ready-to-wear F/W 2018/2019.

to more sober, depending on the colour combined with it. Environmental concerns of the decade led to an uptake in earthy colours, and tangerine was combined with the olives and browns found in nature. Golden browns and burnt oranges were weaved together for preppy plaids and tweeds, representing the colour of autumn leaves on Ivy League campuses, or in muted flower-print patterns on boho maxi dresses.

In the 1970s, orange was also considered a unisex colour, suitable for both boys and girls, at a time when pink was rejected by the feminist movement for pigeonholing women into fixed gender roles. It was considered a happy colour for children's anoraks, toys and playsuits, and so it occupied a space that pink and blue would later fill from the mid 1980s onwards, when children's goods became more gendered.

Orange branding

Because orange readily attracts the eye, it is regularly used for business branding and in advertising. It was the identifiable symbol of budget airline EasyJet, notable for the cheery but garish uniforms of their flight attendants.

As the signature colour of Hermès, orange is also tied to luxury fashion, with the coveted orange gift box as a status symbol. But at the founding of the company in Paris in 1880, the packaging was cream with a golden border, then beige with a brown detail. During the Second World War, with shortages of supplies across France, the cardboard supplier only had orange left, forcing Hermès to change their branding. From then on, it stuck. Carrying the orange box was a sign that one had purchased their exclusive handbags, including the famous Kelly bag, named in honour of Grace Kelly, Princess of Monaco, or the orange leather Birkin bag, designed with actress Jane Birkin.

In 2004, Hermès launched limited-edition orange-dyed goatskin MetroCard sleeves to mark 100 years of the

New York subway. Only 250 of the covers were produced, embossed with the words "Subway Centennial." The *New York Times* posed the question: "So does anyone who shops at Hermès actually ride the subway? Maybe, maybe not. At the party on Thursday more than one person was overheard saying something like, 'This must be the first time in history that the words 'subway' and 'Hermès' have been used in the same sentence.'"

Orange is also linked with Princeton University, considered the most Waspish and fashion-conscious of the United States's Ivy League universities. Orange and black were first recorded as Princeton's signature colours at a baseball game in 1867, after a freshman called George Ward suggested orange be adopted to represent William of Orange, after whom the university's first building had been named.

In 1868, students were permitted to wear the college badge of an orange ribbon with the word "Princeton" in black. These colours were adopted officially in 1896, and the class jacket in the distinctive orange and black was first introduced in 1912. Reunion jackets, given to alumni to wear on the 25th anniversary, have featured bold orange in a number of guises, from black, cream and orange stripes in 1904 to a bright orange with black lapels and buttons in 1916, and tiger stripes in 1965, in tribute to the university mascot and football team.

The prison jumpsuit

When Piper Kerman wrote her 2010 memoirs of her time in prison, she called it *Orange is the New Black*, as a reference to her status as a privileged, fashion-conscious woman forced into the orange jumpsuit of the penitentiary system. Kerman described the moment in prison that inspired the title of her book. One day, she received a letter from a friend who included a clipping of Bill Cunningham's "On the Street" fashion column from the Sunday edition of the *New York Times*. It featured a series of women of all ages, races and sizes dressed in orange, with the headline "Oranginas Uncorked".

Kerman wrote: "I carefully stuck the clipping inside my locker door, where every time I opened it I was greeted by my dear friend's handwriting, and the smiling faces of women with orange coats, hats, scarves, even baby carriages. Apparently, orange was the new black."

Despite the title of her book, in reality, orange is worn in the US prison system only by those who are in transit or have yet to be fully incarcerated. The normal attire in a correctional facility was khaki pants and a top, like hospital scrubs, with black work shoes. It was only when she was sent to the federal prison in Chicago at the end of her correctional sentence that she was issued with "ill-fitting orange men's jumpsuits" which made her feel "a little self-conscious".

Orange has become the prison colour because it's memorable in the way it stands out – those images of orange-clad prisoners at Guantanamo Bay, or the dangerous criminals in the movie *Con Air* (1997). In the nineteenth century, prisoners wore black and white stripes, which became notorious in their connection to chain gangs. Prison uniforms were designed to look distinctive, so that it would make them more visible when they were carrying out work details, or if they absconded. Rather than distinctive stripes, different states began to introduce plain uniforms in grey, brown or green, but it wasn't until the 1970s that the orange prison suit made an appearance, being used in temporary facilities or for transit. Orange became pervasive because it was the visual symbolism of a prisoner when seen in public, either in court, or being transported to other facilities.

Following the global success of *Orange is the New Black* on Netflix, it was reported that one Michigan prison, Saginaw County Jail, changed the uniform of their inmates from oranges to stripes, because civilians were wearing orange jumpsuits and tunics and trousers as a fancy-dress costume. Sheriff William Federspiel told MLive.com that "some people think it's cool to look like an inmate of the Saginaw County Jail with wearing all-orange jumpsuits out at the mall or in public. It's a concern because we do have our inmates out sometimes doing work in the public, and I don't want anyone to confuse them or have them walk away."

Dystopian orange

Just as yellow is used for safety reasons, orange was adopted for lifejackets, buoys, and reflective workwear because of its visibility at night and in fog. In the film *Back to the Future* (1985), hip teenager Marty McFly finds himself travelling back in time in a DeLorean to 1955, the year his parents first fell in love. His items of clothing, including a denim jacket, faded jeans, Nike sneakers, Calvin Klein underwear, and a quilted orange body warmer, are used as punchlines throughout the movie, where the fashions of the 1980s seem mystifying to those in the 1950s.

Marty pulls on his body warmer when meeting Doc Emmett Brown at the mall at midnight, as it is something easy, warm and hi-vis for skateboarding in the dark. Once he's transported back to the 1950s, this vest is frequently mistaken for a life preserver. On entering Hill Valley's diner, the owner, Lou, asks him: "What did you do, jump ship?" One of Biff Tannen's gang also makes a joke: "Get a load of this guy's life preserver. Dork thinks he's gonna drown!" And when he finds himself in the childhood home of his mother, Lorraine, her mother Stella believes he's in the coast guard, asking how long he will be in port. It wasn't until the 1960s that the body warmer, or gilet, first appeared as an item of sportswear for wearing as an extra layer while skiing, and the orange colour was chosen to be visible on the slopes.

The orange hazmat suit also uses colour for visibility, creating an image of dystopia through its use in popular culture. It's become a well-worn trope in movies, with the slow movements of the figure encased in an astronaut-style suit, sucking air through a breathing apparatus. This was nodded to in *Armageddon* (1988), with the crew led by Bruce Willis and Ben Affleck filmed in slow motion, striding across the tarmac in orange space suits as they prepare to hurtle into the stratosphere to save the world.

As Sirin Kale wrote in the *Guardian* in March 2020, in an article on the popularity of hazmat suits in television and film: "Part of the reason that the hazmat suit is so useful to film-makers is because it makes visible what cannot be seen to the naked eye: the threat to life posed by disease." While the colours of the hazmat suit depend on the manufacturer and where they will be used, orange is one of the most popular of these visual signifiers, as it stands out against everything else and acts as a clear warning sign against danger.

For Calvin Klein's Fall 2018 collection, head designer Raf Simons created a dystopian vision on the floor of the American Stock Exchange, covered in a drift of popcorn, as models crunched their way down the runway in burnt-orange hazmat suits, white waders and knitted balaclavas. As Adam Tschorn of the *Los Angeles Times* noted on 14 February 2018: "Once the show started, the parade of orange hazmat suits, balaclavas and chunky round-toed utility boots made it clear. This was a future vision of the American Midwest where global warming – or perhaps nuclear war – had caused the fields of corn to pop en masse. The models representing the workers charged with cleaning up the environmental disaster were clad in the collection's workwear-meets-Western-wear hazmat chic".

Prada's Autumn 2018 collection featured tweed skirts worn with orange nylon jackets with clip-on name tags and orange shoe covers, as if the wearers were entering a laboratory. This trend for dystopian style, elevating the orange hazmat into a fashion item, captured the mood of the times. It fed into the sense of worry and stress around political instability, protests on the street and climate change. Global anxiety would reach its peak during the Covid-19 pandemic in 2020, when the orange hazmat suit, featured in the disaster movie *Outbreak* (1995), seemed all the more appropriate.

Despite the dystopian connotations of hazmat suits, and a sometimes garish quality when combined with other colours, orange represents warmth, confidence and happiness. Alongside Gen Z yellow and millennial pink, orange made a comeback in the age of Instagram as a bold, extroverted choice. Fashion writer Laura Craik wrote in *The Times* on 19 November 2011: "A fashion-lover wouldn't wear DayGlo orange leggings; a fashionista would." When the actress Anya Taylor-Joy was photographed in *Wonderland* magazine in 2020, encased in a bright orange coat by Bottega Veneta, the shoot reinforced the idea that wearing orange is still risk-taking, and often done only by the most fashion-forward. Taylor-Joy also wore dazzling orange at the Venice Film Festival in 2021.

While orange is a colour that connects us to the exquisite citrus fruit, and the symbolism of love and fertility as seen in the works of Botticelli and the Pre-Raphaelites, it's also a colour that has traditionally been considered difficult to wear. Whether it's clashing with purples and browns in the 1960s and 1970s, or standing out like a warning sign on hazmat suits and prison jumpsuits, one thing is for sure – it will always make an impact.

1. Anya Taylor Joy at the Venice Film Festival 2021.

2. Taylor Schilling as Piper Chapman in *Orange is the New Black* (2013–2019).

3. Gigi Hadid, New York, 2018.

Brown is one of nature's dominant colours. Its earthy, rich tones create a sense of warmth and homeliness, from dark wood interiors to the natural tones of leather and suede, and the comfort of tweed jackets, traditionally woven in a range of shades that could blend into the golden, bracken-covered grouse moors of Scotland. It can also be a muddled colour. As Derek Jarman writes in his book on colour, *Chroma* (1993), "No monochromatic wavelength exists for brown. Brown is a sort of darkened yellow." Mixing together the primary colours of red, yellow and blue creates a range of tertiary colours, from beige, taupe, tan, chestnut, and rust to those with tempting, comforting names – chestnut, cocoa, coffee, mocha, latte, toffee, caramel. All those shades and tones of brown are considered neutrals, dependable colours that can act as a support for bolder, brighter colours or, when combined with green or orange, convey nature and wholesomeness.

Brown

The Bar Hemingway at the Ritz Hotel in Paris is a haze of brown; it's fitted with wooden panels, tables and chairs to create a sense of old-fashioned glamour, a place of escape from the chi-chi fashion of the rest of the hotel, where the ghost of the writer Ernest Hemingway still lingers; it was one of his favourite bars. Muted tones were also beloved of the first celebrity decorator, Elsie de Wolfe. When she cast her eyes on the Parthenon in Athens for the first time, she was enraptured by the natural stone: "It's beige! My colour!" For Coco Chanel, beige was reminiscent of nature. "I take refuge in beige because it's natural. Not dyed," she once said, and she incorporated it into her collections as one of her key colours.

Traditionally, brown has been a common shade for trousers, whether it's the buff breeches and pantaloons of the Regency era, the khakis that epitomize Ivy League style, or a pair of geek chic vintage cords. Brown is considered dependable and serious, but it can also be thought boring and lacking in sophistication. The Oxford professor in a tweed jacket, with his brown leather elbow patches, or the businessman who wears a brown suit to work, are often denigrated for their fashion sense.

It's not a colour regularly seen on the red carpet. However, exceptions include Julia Roberts in a simple and understated Armani gown at the Academy Awards in 1990, Halle Berry in chocolate-brown Valentino at the 2002 ceremony, or Gwyneth Paltrow in sheer Fendi at the 2020 Golden Globes. Despite these connotations, there is also a sinister connection to brown. The Nazi *Sturmabteilung*, or "Assault Division", were the paramilitary wing of the rising Nazi party in the 1920s and 1930s, fitted out in leftover brown uniforms from the First World War. Effectively working as hired thugs, they were collectively known as the "Brownshirts". In their uniform, they became a threatening mass of colour unity, much like the blackshirts of Benito Mussolini's National Fascist Party in Italy.

But above all, shades of brown permeate some of fashion's key pieces: the camel coat, an innovation of the brand Jaeger, and Burberry's beige trench coat – both central to the Ivy League style – and the khaki of the army, which later was adapted into a fashion in its own right. But before it had its moment in fashion, brown was a colour worn by the poorest of society.

A pauper's fabric

Because strong, expensive dyes like red, purple and black were preserved for the rich through the decree of sumptuary laws introduced in the Middle Ages, brown fabric was relegated to the lowliest of people, along with greys and washed-out yellows and greens. It wasn't a colour that would lend itself to luminescent brilliance, like Tyrian purple, or evoke wealthy splendour like red. Instead, it often appeared drab and dull.

An early way of dyeing cloth brown was to rub it with minerals and earth elements like ochre and iron rust which would be bound to the fabric with tree resin, saliva, and urine. The iron compounds found in mordants, which fix natural dyes to fabric, also darken fabric brown and black when combined with plant tannins – a method used by the ancient Egyptians from the fourteenth century BCE. There were few recipes for brown in dyers' manuals from the Middle Ages, signifying that there wasn't the same demand for creating browns as there was for the strong blacks and reds that were considered so prestigious.

Brown was mostly associated with the cheap, rough fabrics reserved for the poorest of society. In 1363, in the reign of Edward III, a sumptuary law was introduced by parliament stipulating that paupers could only wear a rough wool cloth known as russet, which was used for hose and doublets. The law stated that the lowliest should "not take nor wear no Manner of Cloth, but Blanket and Russet of Twelve-pence".

Writer Thomas Hardy was nostalgic for the rural life of his childhood in the 1840s and early 1850s, and he wrote wistfully of the traditional styles of peasant dress in his novels, often comparing their rustic clothes to the landscape and linking their environments with clothing, as they become part of nature. In *The Return of the Native* (1878), Hardy describes Clym Yeobright, cutting furze on Egdon Heath, as appearing to be a "russet hue, not more distinguishable from the scene around him than the green caterpillar from the leaf it feeds on", and that the heath appeared as if wearing an "antique brown dress". In *The Woodlanders* (1887), the trees are clothed in "jackets of lichen and stockings of moss", and in *Far from the Madding Crowd* (1874) he compares "soft brown mosses" to "faded velveteen".

The word "beige" first came into use in the nineteenth century, borrowing from the French word for a cloth made from undyed sheep's wool as it came to represent a pale, fawny-brown colour, and later served as a derogatory descriptor for somebody, or something, considered bland and boring.

The idea of wearing natural wool dates back to the Vikings, who are believed to have chosen soft, naturally beige or brown wools for socks, undergarments, leggings and mittens, using a crochet technique known as *nålebinding*. The wool was crucial to the Vikings' way of life, ensuring they kept warm on long sea journeys – and the technique of *nålebinding* was still used by Norwegian seamen into the twentieth century.

As horror stories around the toxicity of aniline dyes were disseminated in the public in the late nineteenth century, the beige and browns of peasant cloth appealed to the dress reformers who wished for a return to healthy, natural clothing that wouldn't poison the wearer. *Health Culture* (1887), a book by German naturalist Dr Gustav Jaeger, featured his essays on health reform. He offered sage advice on tackling disease and maintaining respiratory health, such as leaving the bedroom window open and following his "Sanitary Woollen System". He believed natural, undyed – rather than synthetically dyed – wool should be worn against the skin, and that natural brown wool, rather than white, was far superior in terms of health, because the wool on white sheep was likely to be adulterated, or made possible through unnatural selective breeding. Included in his book was the cautionary tale of a young woman who danced all night in uncomfortable shoes and synthetic stockings. The poison of the dye entered into her blood via the cuts on her feet, causing her to have both feet amputated in order to save her life.

In a series of bizarre experiments, he tested the effects of a variety of dyed clothing on the body's nerves, comparing black clothing with lighter brown by measuring his reaction time in stopping a stopwatch and also in how far he could run. He found that for both experiments, the brown suit gave him faster reaction times, and allowed him to run further, than the dark suits dyed with indigo or logwood. In 1884, English businessman Lewis Tomalin founded Dr Jaeger's Sanitary Woollen System Company Limited to begin manufacturing items in line with Dr Jaeger's teachings. This philosophy, and the favouring of brown tones, grew into the brand Jaeger, which promoted wool and animal fibres for health and warmth, from the brown wool suit to natural wool undergarments and the camel coat.

Beige and buff in the eighteenth century

Following her marriage to the 5th Duke of Devonshire in 1774, 17-year-old Lady Georgiana Spencer became an overnight sensation for her beauty and wit – and her eye for fashion. Whatever she wore was reported in the newspapers and adopted by women in London and Paris. She introduced a demand for three-foot feathers for headdresses, for wearing comical ornaments nestled in hair

1. *Georgiana, Duchess of Devonshire* (1783) by Thomas Gainsborough.

2. Advertisement for Jaeger's camel coats, 1940s.

3. Charles and Diana, the Prince and Princess of Wales, on honeymoon at Balmoral, 1981.

towers, and she also introduced the colour "Devonshire brown" into the lexicon.

With her influence as a leading political hostess, the Duchess of Devonshire was aligned with the more progressive, democratic-leaning Whig party and wore beige and blue to campaign for them and their leader, Charles James Fox. She even chose the colours for the uniform of her statuesque footmen at Chatsworth House. The beige pantaloons and breeches of the Whig party would impact on men's fashion, becoming an essential component of the male uniform, representing the modernity of the pro-American political party.

With a rise in interest in sports and outdoor pursuits in the eighteenth century, and as a reaction against elaborate, fussy fashions, simpler, rough cloth in natural browns was adopted by the wealthy for wearing outdoors. It was what the novelist Honoré de Balzac referred to in 1798 as the "battle between broadcloth and silk", when the eighteenth-century men's fashion for heavily embroidered *habit à la française*, worn with white stockings and buckle shoes, gave way to a simpler, more rugged style.

Beau Brummell, who set the style standard for gentlemen in the Regency period, took inspiration from his time in the glamorous Prince of Wales's Regiment, the 10th Royal Hussars, from 1794 to 1798. He instigated a streamlined, neoclassical style of tight breeches and pantaloons, a white shirt, starched collar and cravat, a blue military-style coat, and well-polished Hessian boots.

The influence of British armed forces and their overseas campaigns in the late eighteenth century helped to shape this style, where natural leather, in shades of fallow and tan, was incorporated into the streamlined look, from their gloves to their overcoats.

To mimic the lean physique of a Greek god, the men wore their buckskin breeches or buff-coloured wool pantaloons, in the colours of Caucasian flesh, so tight that they went without undergarments beneath. To ensure their legs were suitably muscular, wearers sometimes used padding to enhance the calf. There is a story of some men sitting in a bath of water to shrink-fit their breeches, much like young people in the 1950s and 1960s did with their shrink-fit jeans. These skintight breeches or pantaloons were often described as "inexpressibles" because of their erotic fit, as they highlighted muscular legs and every detail around the crotch.

The story of tweed

On their honeymoon at Balmoral in 1981, and with the world's press watching, the Prince and Princess of Wales posed for photographs surrounded by the idyllic Highlands landscape. Prince Charles wore a kilt in the Rothesay tartan with a moss-green V-neck, while Diana chose a tweed hunting suit designed by Bill Pashley, with the earthy checks creating an overall beige effect. The colours and fabric indicated her acceptance within the Royal Family. Rustic tweeds have been a tradition on country estates for British aristocracy since the nineteenth century, where the colours of the weave took inspiration from the wild, barren landscape and the earthy colours of the bracken and gorse.

Tweed was an essential component in the wardrobe of aristocrats who spent their weekends taking part in country pursuits such as hunting and shooting. It was originally created as a practical fabric produced by Scottish crofters in the Outer Hebrides, but it was Sir Walter Scott who influenced a fashion in the 1830s for gentlemen to wear tweed trousers and shooting jackets as a warm, hardy fabric ideal for outdoor sportswear.

When the modern bicycle was first introduced in the 1890s, cycling was enthusiastically taken up by women because they could independently travel the streets without the need for a carriage, a horse or a male companion. The Rational Dress Society, a feminist movement founded in the 1880s to push for practical clothes for women taking part in outdoor pursuits, actively promoted tweed as a suitable material for their divided skirts, which were controversially close in style to trousers. Tweed, with its muted browns, was more sober than the colourful crinolines and bustles that pervaded Victorian women's fashions, and it was initially met with derision, as it was considered too masculine and brusque for women.

Between the World Wars, with clothes offering more freedom for women, and a relaxed sportswear look for men becoming increasingly common, tweed became widespread in both male and female fashion, for motoring and playing outdoor sports like golf. At that time, the most fashionable man on the planet, Edward VIII, later the Duke of Windsor, made a quality Harris Tweed jacket an essential part of his look, along with his patched shooting suits, plus fours and argyle socks for golf.

The Duke of Windsor's wardrobe, while large, was also frugal, and demonstrated how sturdy a tweed jacket could be – he continued to wear one of his father's Rothesay hunting suits dating from 1897. In 1960, the Duke wrote of his grandfather, Bertie's, generation: "They and my father wore even their tweeds, as they did their other clothes, not with a view to relaxation but as a costume dictated by custom for a particular purpose."

Depicting a member of the CIA in the late 1970s in Iran, Ben Affleck wore a Harris Tweed jacket in the 2012 film *Argo*, a costume decision that was on point for the era. Harris Tweed jackets were worn by US spies throughout the Cold War, as revealed by the real-life spy Tony Mendez, played by Affleck. The tweed jacket was a subtle means of indicating their work in covert international operations against Russia. "That was our uniform," Mendez told the *Guardian* in 2013. "The jackets were representative of our group. Those of us in the CIA who did overseas work, work in the field. If you were in the field during the Blitz, you wore a trench coat. If you were tracking Ivan [the Soviet Union and its allies], you had Harris Tweed."

The tweed jacket is unobtrusive and tends not to attract attention. It's worn by people perceived as being innocuous – professors at university or geography teachers, perhaps, but the variety of weave, with muted browns mixed with oranges and olive greens, adds to the sense of individuality. The fabric gained a cult following when Alexander McQueen, with a strong interest in Scottish heritage fabrics, incorporated tweeds into his designs, including the Alfred Hitchcock–inspired Autumn/Winter 2005/2006 collection.

Incorporated into the "hipster" movement of the new millennium, tweed was worn as an ironic statement. Post-9/11, Millennials, or Generation Y (those born c. 1980 to c. 1995), lived under the shadow of war and terrorism. With this instability and widespread social injustice as the backdrop to their lives, they sought comfort in the look of the past and an appreciation of nature. This intensified even more with the 2008 financial crash and concerns around climate change. Tweed caps, waistcoats and beards spoke of simpler, old-fashioned times, referencing the past, but with a modern twist.

Khaki uniforms
At the outbreak of the First World War in 1914, eager volunteers signed up to the British Army and were equipped with new khaki uniforms. Despite being baggy and ill-fitting on the bodies of these yet-to-be battle-hardened men, young women were so enraptured at the sight of men in uniform that they were said to have "khaki fever". Recruitment posters also shamed young men into signing up by asking, "Why aren't you in khaki?" The khaki of the First World War was more of an olive green than the dusty brown that belied its origins, but its name can imply a colour that ranges from olive to dull brown,

1. Moira Howard in a Rensor tweed coat, London, 1947.

2. Julia Roberts at the 62nd Academy Awards, 1990.

3. Recruitment poster for the Women's Army Corps, 1941–1945.

WOMAN'S PLACE IN WAR
The Army of the United States
has 239 kinds of jobs for women
THE WOMEN'S ARMY CORPS

fawn and beige, depending on which branch of the armed forces had adapted it.

The word "khaki" originated from the Urdu word *khak*, meaning dust, and is believed to have been invented by Sir Harry Lumsden, who raised a Corps of Guides at Peshawar in 1846 and camouflaged their uniforms by rubbing in mud. He called it "drab", and the beige shade was initially achieved on a larger scale by dyeing white cloth with tea, coffee, soil, and even curry powders. From 1885, all regiments in India were issued a khaki uniform of tunic and trousers, as the colour made soldiers far less conspicuous than the previous red-dyed jackets.

When Britain declared war on Germany on 3 September 1939, the National Service (Armed Forces) Act was immediately introduced, and all men between the ages of 18 and 41 were asked to register for the armed forces and to select their branch of choice. After distinguishing themselves in the Battle of Britain in 1940, the RAF, with its prestigious blue uniform and reputation for glamour, was overwhelmingly the most popular, followed by the navy, but it was the army that absorbed the majority of men. The army recruits were issued rough, ill-fitting khaki uniforms, earning them the disparaging nickname "brown jobs", as coined by the men of the RAF, which indicated their status as just another cog in the machine.

While some recruits had to make do with uniforms that had been worn by the "Tommies" of the First World War, the army had introduced in 1938 a new khaki "battledress" consisting of a short blouson jacket and baggy trousers in beige wool serge. This new battledress, considered one of the most efficient of army uniforms, would inspire the US Army's field jacket, introduced once America joined the war in late 1941.

Despite gripes that the jacket and trousers of the battledress came apart, there was a sense of pride in wearing khaki as the soldiers were trained up to be sent to fight in France in 1939. Sergeant John Williams, of the 6th Battalion, Durham Light Infantry, recalled: "We felt sorry for people who weren't in the army. We were having such a good time! We were being soldiers, and all the girls thought we were smart and handsome, and these poor sods were still working in the pit and the office."

Women in the Second World War also signed up to the armed services, and while the blue of the Women's Auxiliary Air Force (WAAF) and the Women's Royal Navy Service (WRNS, known as the Wrens) were the most desirable, those in the Air Transport Auxiliary (ATA) made do with the less prestigious khaki, styled after the Mechanised Transport Corps (MTC) outfit of the First World War. For the 200,000 women who joined the Auxiliary Territorial Service (ATS) during the war, doing work that included driving, typing and administration, cooking, and working on anti-aircraft and searchlight batteries, their khaki uniform was universally considered dowdy and unflattering. Even their stockings were khaki – a marked contrast to the glamorous black stockings of the Wrens. When Princess Elizabeth signed up to the ATS as a driver and mechanic in spring 1945, she gave the khaki some much needed prestige.

The ATS also offered women from deprived backgrounds the chance of a better life. They were given three meals a day, their own bed, and more new clothing than many had owned before. This included three pairs of khaki lock-knit knickers, at a time when owning several pairs of underwear was rare; a belted khaki serge tunic and skirt, lined with khaki cotton; and a khaki shirt and tie. The uniform may have been an undesirable brown-green, and in a dowdy shape, but women pulled in their belts in an attempt to create more of an hourglass silhouette.

While khaki was often derided by those who wore the colour, there was also a sense of cachet, particularly when it was worn by the American soldiers, who imbued it with glamour when they arrived on British shores in 1942. The colour of their uniforms was known as "olive drab", and was worn with a pale brown shirt and tie and a cap.

As a boy watching the build-up to D-Day, historian John Keegan was disappointed that the British soldiers he saw "wore khaki from top to toe ... so ill-cut, shapeless and hairy that I could find almost nothing in its wearers to admire". When the Americans arrived, he and his school friends were amazed at "how different they looked from our own jumble-sale champions, beautifully clothed in smooth khaki". Similarly, Stephanie Batstone, in her memoirs of being a Wren, wrote of dancing with American soldiers at a "Yank dance" in Warrington, where "your hand was on that smooth pale, beautiful cloth, your eye was level with the US shoulder flash ... They had proper shoes, not hobnail boots, and they never trod on your feet".

The Ivy Look

After the Second World War, khaki trousers became a popular part of the Ivy League college campus look, a casual, sporty style that referenced the British aristocratic style with a functional American twist. According to Patricia Mears, deputy director at the Museum at FIT (Fashion Institute of Technology), the term "ivy" was formally established in 1954, during the formation of the National Collegiate Athletic Association Division I conference, with the name growing out of a desire to establish rules governing intercollegiate athletics. It initially represented the four most prestigious universities – Harvard, Yale, Princeton and Columbia – using the Roman numerals IV. Others point to earlier descriptions in novels, some as far back as 1888, of colleges as "ivy-covered" or "ivied".

The Ivy League style filtered into the WASP college campuses in America in the 1920s and 1930s, shaped by British dandy style, and in particular by the future Duke of Windsor, with his Norfolk jackets and tweed suits. While the Ivy League incorporated flourishes of colour, brown was dominant in the palette, from the khaki trousers to the earthy tweed jackets and brown weejun loafers. In the autumn of 1935, the magazine *Apparel Arts* noted the freshman look of a "loose fitting three-button brown herringbone Shetland suit, a cream colored flannel Tattersall waistcoat and brown overcheck".

In the 1960s, young Japanese men appeared on the streets of Tokyo dressed in the Ivy League style, a subculture known as *aibii*, for "Ivy", and decades later, "dad style". In 1965, businessman Shosuke Ishizu was researching how to sell American fashion to the Japanese, but because the style's rules seemed so complicated, he sent a team to the main Ivy League campuses to record it in person. In their observations, listed as essential components for the look were a plain or herringbone tweed jacket, a polo coat in camel, "a raglan-sleeve, polo, or Burberry coat in beige or olive brown" for a raincoat and "a beige golf jacket with poplin, a quilted ski parka, brownish duffle coat".

The Ivy League style would become known as the "preppy" style of all-American designers Ralph Lauren and Tommy Hilfiger, and it would flourish in the 1970s as a rejection of the hippie movement in favour of a classic, more conservative style. When Steve McQueen starred as a macho police detective in *Bullitt* (1968), it heralded a grittier, more urban style of film-making. McQueen played it cool as detective Frank Bullitt in a brown herringbone tweed jacket with black polo neck, and a beige overcoat, sometimes casually slung over his shoulder. His co-star Jacqueline Bisset was in synergy with his style, wearing a functional, but offbeat, wardrobe, including a camel coat with roll-neck.

The popularity of the Ivy League style was also aided by the film *Love Story*, released in 1970. Ryan O'Neal and Ali MacGraw set an international trend for the preppy look in their costumes designed by Pearl Somner and Alice

1. Ryan O'Neal and Ali MacGraw in *Love Story* (1970).

2. Olivia Palermo at Paris Fashion Week, September 2019.

3. Robert Redford and Barbra Streisand in *The Way We Were* (1973).

Manougian Martin. The film hit cinemas before the Beatles announced their break-up in early 1970, marking the end of the love-in of the 1960s, and a return to the classic American sportswear style. MacGraw's camel coat, in particular, defined the look of the time, coordinated with O'Neal's beige polo coat, brown sheepskin jacket and chinos as they stroll around campus together, falling in love.

The original camel coat was designed by Jaeger, and was launched in 1919, helping put London on the style map alongside Paris. While the word "camel" accurately indicates the tawny colour, the name of the coat was actually derived from hardy camel hair. An animal that can survive extreme heat during the day and cold nights in the desert, the camel has hair that creates a uniquely durable fabric. During the Second World War, when there was a shortage of silk, leather and wool, the availability of camel hair meant that these coats could be readily supplied, and Jaeger included it in their line of wartime utility clothing. These days, most "camel" coats are made with wool or other natural fibres.

The camel coat was a style staple in films of the late 1960s and 1970s. In the emotional final scene of the drama *The Way We Were* (1973), Barbra Streisand's character is adjusting the collar of her belted camel coat as she spots her former lover, played by Robert Redford, on the streets of New York in a beige trench coat. While they both have new partners, the similar pale browns of their coats link them together, even though they realize they can't reunite. The look is also very 1970s, despite the film being set decades before, but it indicates a timeless quality to the style, and the classic colour. It would go on to inspire French couturier Anne-Marie Beretta, who created the iconic 101801 Max Mara camel cashmere coat in 1981, and opined, "The coat is the first refuge". The simple style, and colour, would become the signatures of the brand, which is known for its classic minimalism.

The trench coat

Another vital element of preppy style was the beige trench coat – made famous by the quintessential British brand Burberry. Thomas Burberry, a country draper, developed a water- and windproof fabric he patented as gabardine, and which first went on sale in the 1890s. Designed for field sports, it was later used by officers in the trenches of the First World War. In the 1920s, when the beige, black and red check plaid of the lining was first introduced, it became a unisex fashion item, and a favourite for androgynous actresses like Greta Garbo and Marlene Dietrich.

At the beginning of the millennium, the distinctive Burberry check became instantly recognizable when it appeared on bikinis, baseball caps and headscarves, shifting its position from its original place as an upmarket brand to a symbol of "chav" style, encouraged by stars like Victoria Beckham being photographed wearing the check.

To reinvent Burberry, bringing it back to a position of exclusivity, Christopher Bailey was hired as creative director in 2004. He reinvigorated a brand that had become staid into one that was synonymous with cool, preserving the classic beige gabardine belted trench coat, but placing it firmly as a unisex item, with actors Cara Delevingne and Eddie Redmayne wearing them for the 2012 campaign, photographed by Mario Testino.

Ugly chic

The 1970s was marked by an uptake of neutrals – browns combined with oranges and greens, which were earthy, traditional and stable at a time of political upheaval and instability. Fashion brand Biba opened their innovative but short-lived Kensington department store in 1973 to great fanfare, which transported customers into sepia-tinted nostalgia, as it replicated the art nouveau style of the Edwardian era. It was described in the *New York Times*: "The set is extraordinary. Deep brown is the dominant color

1. Azzedine Alaïa fashion show in Paris, October 1986.

2. Steve McQueen in *Bullitt* (1968).

3. Michelle Obama at the White House dinner for the Indian prime minister, 2009.

and tan mirrors cover the counters, reflecting the mocha lights and the carpets that cover everything, even the waste baskets."

Evoking the 1970s look but with a 90s twist, British indie band Pulp made an indelible impact on pop culture with the smash success of their single 'Common People' in 1995. Lead singer Jarvis Cocker invented the geek chic look, with his jumble-sale aesthetic of brown tweed jackets, cords and garish polyester shirts. The style was picked up by Prada for the Spring/Summer 1996 collection, officially named "Banal Eccentricity", but dubbed "ugly chic". Models Kate Moss and Amber Valletta walked the catwalk in a 1970s silhouette of A-line skirts and wide-lapelled shirts, with geometric patterns that mixed muddy brown with citron, aubergine and rust. "Ugly is in," wrote Robin D. Givhan of the show in the *Washington Post* in May 1996. She described how the colours "hovered somewhere between shades of slime and mold. The browns were murky – the color of water as it stagnates over a long, steamy summer."

Nude tones
For Azzedine Alaïa's Spring/Summer 1987 collection, models gathered on the streets of Paris in stretchy, figure-hugging dresses which would become known as the "body-con" look. In varying shades of creams and brown, the garments blended with the skin tones of the models.

"Nude" or "flesh-toned" are often used to describe a pale peachy brown, said to blend in with the skin, but it's limiting in that it only refers to white skin. A controversy around the terminology bubbled up when First Lady Michelle Obama wore a cream-coloured dress, decorated with a silver flower motif, by designer Naeem Khan, at a state dinner for the Indian prime minister in November 2009. When the Associated Press labelled it as "flesh-coloured", it sparked widespread criticism, and they rushed to update the description to "champagne". A *Guardian* article in May 2010 posed the question, "Nude: is the hot fashion colour racist?", while the media website Jezebel asked, "Nude? For whom?"

"Nude" was a major trend in 2010, dominating the spring and summer collections, and featuring in the fashion editorials of major publications. In its May 2010 issue, *Elle* magazine declared, "nude is *the* colour for spring/summer".

"It isn't just the description of a colour that is potentially offensive here, it's also the way the look is styled, the conception of the entire trend", wrote Paula Cocozza in the *Guardian* in 2010. "On the catwalks in Paris, Milan, London and New York, these pale shades were presented almost uniformly on pale skins. It's a look that's all about white skin."

Darker skin tones were, for decades, largely ignored by the fashion and beauty industry, until the body positivity movement pushed for diversity and inclusion. As well as campaigning for the visibility of different body shapes, the movement also pushed for make-up to be tailored to all skin tones, and for the words "nude" and "flesh" to be relegated to history.

In recent years, "nude" heels have become a wardrobe staple, favoured by the Duchess of Cambridge, but they were light and beige, rather than reflecting other skin tones. Christian Louboutin was one of the first to address it, with a collection of nude heels in a variety of shades. The peachy, pale pink of ballet slippers was traditionally considered "nude" in colour. In the US, no companies made pointe shoes for darker skin tones until Gaynor Minden in 2017, and in the UK in 2018, when Freed dancewear joined up with the Ballet Black dance company to create an inclusive range of shoes.

When businesswoman Ade Hassan grew frustrated at being unable to find tights or underwear to match her skin, she launched Nubian Skin in 2014, which is now sold in 50 countries around the world. Fenty Beauty, the brand founded by the singer and designer Rihanna, was an overnight sensation when it was launched in September 2017, with foundations and concealers in 40 different shades for long under-represented skin tones. While other companies like MAC Cosmetics had a wide range of shades, Fenty celebrated inclusivity with women of colour in their advertising, and reportedly made $100 million in sales in its first 40 days on the market. *Time* magazine named it one of the 50 Genius Companies of 2018 for "broadening makeup's palette".

Kim Kardashian's Skims line is a range of shapewear undergarments made from nylon and spandex. Despite the purpose of the garments to contour the silhouette, the aim was to make it body positive, using women of all sizes and skin tones. Shapewear traditionally only comes in beige or black, so Kardashian set out to make a range of nine colours for different skin tones. She named the palest "sand", the darkest "onyx", and those in between "ochre", "sienna" and "oxide". "I couldn't find something that would match my skin tone," she told the *New York Times* in 2020. "Let alone, how am I going to find something for my girls when they're older?"

"Brown" covers a range of meanings, from a traditional Victorian aesthetic of tweed jackets in mahogany drawing rooms, to the timelessness of a beige Burberry trench coat or camel coat, which continue to be street-style staples. Brown can be considered dowdy, drab and in bad taste, or it can symbolize health and homeliness, but as the debate around "nude" and "flesh tones" indicates, it's a shade that is wide-ranging and hard to pin down.

When Julie Marsden, a spirited Southern belle
in 1852 New Orleans, defiantly chooses to wear
a shimmering red gown to the Olympus Ball,
when the code for unmarried ladies is strictly
virginal white, she is immediately ostracized by
her community and shames her fiancé, Pres, into
breaking off their engagement. Julie, the fictional
lead character played by Bette Davis in 1938's
Jezebel, learns how powerful a red dress can be –
the garment transforms her into a brazen entity.
She metaphorically becomes the Whore of Babylon
– who was depicted in Biblical art dressed in a red
cloak, riding on a red beast – and redeems herself
only by showing complete humility and remorse,
by sacrificing herself to care for Pres in a highly
infectious yellow-fever colony.

Red

Rather than seeing shocking red in vivid Technicolor, the black and white film only implies the colour through a particular shade of grey. In reality, the costume designer Orry-Kelly used a lustrous rust-brown fabric to create the illusion – but Julie's bold actions, followed by her shame, mean that all we can see is red. The idea for the red gown, standing out like a slash of blood on pristine white, was said to have been inspired by a real-life Hollywood incident from 1936. At the Mayfair Ball that year, where the guest list featured the film industry elite, the hostess Carole Lombard requested that her female guests wear formal gowns of snowy white, without a hint of colour. Making a late entrance was actress Norma Shearer, wife of MGM executive Irving Thalberg, dressed in an eye-catching scarlet gown. Always one to refuse to be outdone in the glamour stakes, she made sure all eyes would be on her.

As gossip columnist Hedda Hopper recalled in 1945:

Then in through the foyer and down the steps of the old Victor Hugo restaurant...where the ball was held, swept Norma Shearer, smiling her pearlies from ear to ear, dead sure that every eye in the house was on no one but her. Because she had on the reddest red evening gown you ever saw. The only spot of fiery color in the whole place!

There was one mass gasp. People were stunned and shocked. I saw Carole turn whiter than the holy-white dress she wore. Then she turned and walked out of the place. I saw a tall, dark and extremely handsome guy hurry after her. He followed her out the door and he took her home. His name was Clark Gable. That was the night their romance really began.

Red represents a warning sign, like the flash of a siren and a traffic stop, or James Dean's windbreaker in *Rebel without a Cause* (1955), and the woman who wears it becomes the only one we see in the room. When Cameron Diaz makes her film debut in *The Mask* (1994), in a figure-hugging red dress slashed to the thigh, she uses her clothing as a diversion as she helps to plan a bank robbery, just as a woman wearing a red dress is used to distract Neo in 1999's *The Matrix*. From Jessica Rabbit in *Who Framed Roger Rabbit* (1988) to Michelle Pfeiffer in *The Fabulous Baker Boys* the following year, the woman wearing red captures attention – and double takes. The clothing she wears indicates that she is in complete command of her sensuality.

Because red is so attention-grabbing, it's often considered inappropriate or tacky, like the red dress at the all-white ball. In *The Bride Wore Red* (1937), Joan Crawford plays a cabaret singer, Anni, who pretends to be an aristocrat at a chalet resort, as part of a *Pygmalion*-style bet. Anni has always dreamt of wearing a red dress, matching her desire to make a better life for herself. Unaware of the customs of high society, her chambermaid warns her against wearing it – "Not this red dress, not here" – but Anni doesn't listen and chooses her moment to make her entrance in red. The gown is a spectacular creation by MGM's costume designer, Adrian, sparkling with hand-sewn ruby-red bugle beads. But she realizes the dress is "too loud, and too cheap", and only serves to bring the wrong kind of attention.

Little Red Riding Hood

Perhaps the most famous red piece of clothing in literature, and one of the oldest, is the scarlet cloak or hood belonging to Little Red Riding Hood. The fable of the girl in red, her grandmother and the big bad wolf dates back to around 1023, as an oral tale by Egbert, the Bishop of Liège.

In his 1697 version of the story, *Le Petit Chaperon Rouge*, Charles Perrault described Little Red Riding Hood as "the prettiest creature was ever seen", who wore a red riding hood that had been made for her by her doting grandmother. The red of her costume is a marker of her sexuality, acting as a warning to young girls not to talk to the strange men who may prey on her. The 1812 Brothers Grimm tale ends with the words, "Red-Cap thought to herself, 'As long as I live, I will never by myself leave the path, to run into the wood, when my mother has forbidden me to do so.'" The red also reflects the traditional practice for a girl who is celebrating a holiday or travelling to visit a beloved relative; she would be dressed in her best clothing, which for girls in the Middle Ages was red.

The symbolic power of red is common in literature, tales and legends, and in fairy tales in particular, red was often mentioned alongside white and black. In *Little Red Riding Hood*, red is the colour of her hood, black is the wolf, and white is the butter (or cake, depending on which version of the story you read) she is carrying. The three colours also feature in the Brothers Grimm fairytale *Snow White*, when the titular character's mother wishes for a child "as white as snow, as red as blood, and as black as the wood in this frame".

Red, white and black were the three primal colours first acknowledged by humans. They were used in early cave paintings and art, and adopted by the Christian church as a triad of colours. As the first examples of colour symbolism, red represented blood and life; black, darkness; and white, purity and the Holy Spirit. And out of these three colours, red is considered the first "real" colour because it has a defined wavelength, as opposed to white, which reflects all colours, and black, which absorbs them.

The power of red
Red held powerful significance for the ancient Egyptians, both negative and positive. It symbolized the burning of the sun, and violence and destruction, alongside Set, the god of war and chaos, who was often portrayed as a red-haired beast. Red also signified blood, power and life, exemplified

1. *Court Ladies Adorning Their Hair With Flowers* (c. ninth century CE) by Zhou Fang.

2. German illustration of Little Red Riding Hood in *Grimms' Fairy Tales*.

3. *Portrait of Eleanor of Toledo* (c.1543) by Agnolo Bronzino.

through Isis, goddess of fertility, who was often depicted wearing a red girdle. *Tyet* amulets, made from red jasper, carnelian or red glass to symbolize drops of Isis's blood, were believed to protect the wearer with her magic. The *tyet* was also known as the Isis knot and resembled that of the cloth used to absorb menstrual blood, linking red with the life-giving power of women.

Similarly, in the Palaeolithic era, red was thought to have protective, mystical qualities. Red ochre-painted pieces of bone and teeth to make amulets, necklaces and bracelets have been found in burial places. In the Roman era, red fabric and jewels were also placed in tombs, with the ruby as the most prized. It was thought to warm the body, arouse sexual desire, stimulate the mind and keep away poisonous creatures.

At a traditional Chinese New Year or wedding celebration, you'll find strings of red lanterns, and red paper envelopes given as favours. Red is an auspicious color in China as the symbol of joy, luck and celebration, and a red dress and red veil were traditionally worn by brides on their wedding day to drive away evil spirits. Similarly, in Hindu culture, red is a customary colour for weddings to bring prosperity, fertility, purity, and passion to a marriage, with the groom in a red turban and bride in a red sari, with a red bindi fixed to her forehead.

The most enduring connotations of red are fire and blood, both of which are the ultimate symbol of power as they stimulate both life and death. Early Christianity connected red to the destructive flames of hell, to devils and demons, but by the twelfth and thirteenth centuries, red came to symbolize the blood of Christ, and was worn by cardinals in Rome for their cloaks and caps. Red was also worn by judges, and those working in law, to represent justice. As Michel Pastoureau writes in *Red: The History of a Color* (2016): "The red of power, the red of sin, the red of punishment, the red of blood to be shed: we will find this symbolism for the colour lasting well into the modern period."

The history of red dyeing

In the ancient world, red dye was created predominantly from two substances: the root of the madder plant, and the dried bodies of female insects known as kermes, named from the Persian for "red", and these would continue to be the dominant source of red dye throughout the Renaissance and up until the Spanish colonization of the Americas.

The pinkish roots of the madder plant, also known as *Rubia tinctorum*, is one of the oldest, and most widely used substances to be cultivated for dyeing fabrics. Textile fragments excavated from the Timna Valley in southern Israel, dating from the eleventh to tenth century BCE, were found to have been dyed red from madder.

Kermes, often mistaken for tiny specks of wheat or seeds, which gave it the name "grain" in European languages, were traded extensively throughout the classical world, and in the first century CE, Pliny the Elder noted that "the red, that of the kermes" is first among "fabrics which rival the colours of flowers". Extracting dye from these tiny insects, which fed on the sap of the oak tree, was a laborious process. The red dye only came from the female, and she had to be captured at the moment she was preparing to lay her eggs. The bugs were then dried in the sun and crushed to secrete their red juice, and it took a large haul of insects to obtain even a small amount of dye.

From the second century BCE, safflower was used to dye silk in China and East Asia to create red and blush tones for exquisite gowns, as depicted in a silk scroll from the early ninth-century CE, Zhou Fang's *Court Ladies Adorning Their Hair with Flowers*. While safflower could fade quickly, it wasn't until the nineteenth century that cochineal or *yang hong* ("foreign red"), was made widely available. For the Japanese, red symbolized luxury and sensuality, and it was overwhelmingly achieved through the use of safflower and Japanese madder. There was one exception: high-ranking samurai in the eighteenth century wore a sleeveless jacket, or *jimbaori*, made from valuable imported red wool from Europe, which had been dyed with cochineal and fixed with a tin mordant.

None of these red dyes could compete with the cochineal of the Americas, an insect that fed on the prickly pear cactus and created the brightest, most fade-resistant reds that had ever been discovered. Like kermes, the dye was extracted by drying the female insects in the sun and soaking them in water, but it created 10 times the amount of colourant and supplanted all other red dyes for desirability.

The Inca, who ruled a vast region from northern Ecuador to southern Chile from the 1430s until 1532 CE, associated red with the ancient and mythical origins of religion and culture. Mama-Ocllo, the first Inca queen who helped originally populate the earth, is said to have emerged from the cave of origin wearing a red dress. Cochineal-dyed garments had a vital place in the culture, where they acted as signals to the gods. During the ritual of *capacocha*, young women dressed in red and white garments were sacrificed to Ilyapa, the god of thunder.

Túpac Amaru, the last of the Incan royal family, was marched in chains into the central plaza of Cuzco by the Spanish invaders in 1572, where he was to be executed. He was dressed in the Spanish-style mantle and doublet of cochineal-dyed velvet, but on his head was the royal headdress, the *mascapaychu*, with the red fringe over his forehead. He was led to the scaffold to be hanged, and the 15,000-strong crowd cried out in anguish as they witnessed the end of the Inca civilization and the last ruler wearing the powerful red headdress.

In 1500, kermes was Europe's most valuable source of red dye. By the end of the century, it had been replaced by cochineal. It became one of the Spanish Empire's most lucrative commodities, along with plundered gold, as they swept through the continent and took the land from the indigenous peoples. By the mid sixteenth century, Spanish flotillas brought 125 to 150 tons a year of the dried insects to Europe from the Americas. Because of their expensive bounty, Spanish ships were targeted by pirates and English galleons. One of Elizabeth I's favourite courtiers, Robert Devereux, the second Earl of Essex, captured a large quantity of cochineal in 1597, and shortly after posed for his portrait dressed in a rich scarlet robe.

Shipments of cochineal were traded from Spain to the Netherlands and France, and from Mexico to the Philippines and along the silk routes to the Middle East. Cochineal was used to create the luxurious Venetian velvets from the mid sixteenth century, to dye English wool for the British redcoat uniforms in Amsterdam's lucrative dyeing factories, and to create a rouge to blush the cheeks of aristocratic ladies.

The first printed book on the technicalities of dyeing, published in Venice in 1548, was *The Plictho Of Gioanventura Rosetti*. His recipes for red dye referred to kermes and madder, rather than cochineal, to achieve the Venetian reds that were so important in Renaissance Italy. He also included recipes using extracts of brazilwood, imported from the American tropics, which created pink tones or could be added as a supplement to boost madder. While there had at first been restrictions on its use, cochineal was widespread in Italy by the late sixteenth century, particularly for dyeing cardinals' red cloaks and caps. Madder continued to be used as a less expensive alternative.

By the eighteenth century, in the textile centre of Amsterdam, dyers created garments in both deep, purply crimson and brilliant, orangey scarlet by adding salts and even turmeric to the cochineal dye bath. Jean Hellot, in 1789's *Art of Dying Wool, Silk and Cotton*, described "fire scarlet" as "tinged with orange ... fiery red and dazzling ... Cochineal, which produced this beautiful colour, and which is called Meztique or Texcale, is an insect gathered in considerable quantity in Mexico."

During the period of Enlightenment from 1715, dark reds went out of fashion in favour of peachy pinks, cornflower blues and lemon yellows, as French court fashions became the dominant style across Europe. Yet, for the poorer classes, women continued to save their best red dress for holidays and celebrations, while men commonly wore madder-dyed trousers – an example of fashions filtering downwards.

When German chemists Carl Graebe and Carl Liebermann, along with British chemist William Perkin, discovered in 1868 how to create synthesized alizarin, a red dye, the price of madder steadily declined, as it was now possible to create madder red without the use of natural dyes. It was followed by "fuchsine", a rich crimson discovered by French chemist François-Emmanuel Verguin in 1859. This was renamed "magenta", after the victorious battle of Napoleon III against the Austrian Empire, and for the next decade was one of the most fashionable of the brilliant chemical hues of the time. "Congo red", discovered in 1884 by Paul Böttiger, was the first dye that could be fixed directly to cotton without the use of a mordant.

Despite the developments in synthetic dye, madder was used to dye the red trousers and caps of French infantrymen when they signed up for war in the summer of 1914. Their uniforms remained unchanged from 1870, and the colour made them an easy target for the Germans against the muted landscape of the battlefield. By spring 1915, after suffering a huge loss of life, the French Army abandoned their madder-dyed trousers for a less conspicuous uniform.

Red of the Renaissance

First printed in Paris in 1495, *Le Blason des Couleurs en Armes, Livrées et Devises*, an anonymously authored guide to the colours of heraldry, noted:

> Among the virtues, red signifies noble birth, honour, valour, generosity and daring. It is also the colour of justice and charity, in memory of our Lord Jesus Christ. Combined with other colours, red ennobles them. On a piece of clothing, it gives great courage to the one who wears it. Paired with green, red is beautiful and signifies youth and joie de vivre. With blue, wisdom and fidelity. With yellow, avarice and greed. Red does not go well with black, but with grey, it is the sign of great hopes. And with white, these are two very beautiful colours, signs of the highest virtues.

In the Middle Ages, red was a beloved colour. For men, it represented power and glory, worn in war and for hunting, and for women, it represented beauty and love. A red dress was designed to appeal and attract, and at medieval tournaments, a lady would give her expensively dyed red sleeve to a knight as a token of love, which was said to bring luck when tied to his lance. England in the Middle Ages was a powerhouse of wool production. When Europe began trading with the powerful West African kingdom of Benin from the fifteenth century, scarlet wool was greatly treasured. It was a fabric and colour fit for royals, with only the king being able to grant permission for lesser subjects to wear it.

Because of the expense of creating vivid crimson and scarlet, and its desirability as a symbol of elegance and beauty, red was regulated throughout Europe for only the highest-ranking citizens. Sumptuary laws had been in place since 1337 with two purposes: to protect the domestic economy by limiting imports, and to protect

1. Joan Crawford in *The Bride Wore Red* (1937).

2. Michelle Pfeiffer in *The Fabulous Baker Boys* (1989).

the class system, by ensuring everyone knew their place. Luxury red textiles, created using kermes rather than madder, were referred to as *escarlate*, or "scarlet", which had been a term originally describing an expensive cloth from fine wool. Because these fabrics were most often red, the word came to define the colour.

By the Renaissance period, red had replaced purple as the colour of royalty and power in Italy, and only certain privileged people could wear the colour. In 1558, for example, women from Pistoia were forbidden from wearing cloth dyed with kermes, as were married women in Florence. Because of their expense, Venetian scarlets dyed with kermes were reserved only for the elite. The facilities for dyeing madder and kermes were kept separate, to ensure there was no mixing between the two different qualities of dye. Red was often relegated to prostitutes, lepers and convicts, to mark them out as outcasts of society, with a madder- or brazilwood-dyed cap or scarf.

In his frescoes, Domenico Ghirlandaio depicted Florence's most prominent citizens dressed in fine red clothing in scenes from the Bible. In *The Visitation* (1491), the ladies are dressed in blush-coloured gowns and cloaks, while in *The Expulsion of Joachim from the Temple*, from a few years before, the gentlemen wear a red cloak and hat. Titian was also a great painter of reds, creating subtle shades and tones ranging from delicate pink to burgundy using vermillion, the pigment from cinnabar. In *The Assumption of the Virgin* (1516–18), Mary holds focus in a red gown as she rises up to heaven.

Eleanor of Toledo, the Spanish wife of Cosimo de' Medici, the second Duke of Florence, was trusted by her husband to look after his business while he travelled. With her philanthropy and her own business interests, she was a powerful first lady, and she dressed the part in the most luxurious fashions – the finest silks and velvets often threaded with gold and silver. A 1543 portrait by Agnolo

Bronzino depicts her wearing a silk gown of deep red, embroidered with gold and studded with pearls. She was also famed for the red silk stockings that she chose to wear every day. Following her death from malaria at the age of 40, Eleanor was buried in her red stockings, and in a red dress similar to the one depicted in the Bronzino portrait. One of the only surviving dresses from Florence in the time period of 1540 to 1580 is held at the Museo Nazionale di Palazzo Reale, in Pisa. It is a rich red velvet gown in a similar style to Eleanor's burial dress.

In the English royal courts, as in Renaissance Italy, red fabric was favoured for royalty because of the expense of achieving a deep red dye from the kermes. Henry VII was never meant to be king – his defeat of Richard III in 1485 was unexpected – and so, to cement his status as rightful ruler, he splashed out on clothing for himself and his bride-to-be, Elizabeth of York. In the autumn of 1485, he purchased 10 yards of crimson velvet and 6 yards of russet damask, along with 64 timbers of ermine, so she could have a new wardrobe fit for a Tudor queen.

To make sure he was the most dazzling, impressive figure at court, the next king, Henry VIII, issued a sumptuary law in 1510 that regulated clothing. Purple cloth or gold or purple silk was limited to the king and his direct family, and crimson or blue velvet could be worn only by ranks equal to or above a knight of the garter. As a reward to the henchmen of his ceremonial entourage, Henry issued them coats of crimson velvet, decorated with silver Tudor roses. He also awarded some of his master craftsmen with red wool livery coats and a red woollen cap.

While the Spanish Catherine of Aragon favoured black, Henry VIII's other five wives are often depicted wearing red. In a portrait by Hans Holbein the Younger in 1536, Jane Seymour wears a red velvet gown. His sixth wife, Catherine Parr, was known to be charming and educated, and often dressed in crimson fabrics to complement her auburn hair and pale skin. For the court reception of the Duke of Najera on 18 February 1544, she wore "an open robe of cloth of gold, the sleeves lined with crimson satin, and trimmed with three piled crimson velvet, the train more than two yards long".

The scarlet petticoat

When Mary Queen of Scots was executed on 8 February 1587, her mournful black satin gown was removed to reveal a dark scarlet bodice and petticoat, described in contemporary accounts as being close to rust-brown. As Antonia Fraser described in her 1969 biography of the Stuart queen:

> Stripped of her black, she stood in her red petticoat and it was seen that above it she wore a red satin bodice, trimmed with lace, the neckline cut low at the back; one of her women handed her a pair of red sleeves, and it was thus wearing all red, the colour of blood, and the liturgical colour of martyrdom in the Catholic Church, that the queen of Scots died.

Anne Boleyn similarly wore a crimson petticoat under her loose dark grey gown to her execution two decades before, on 19 May 1536 in the Tower of London. It wasn't solely a symbolic statement for women who were to meet untimely deaths; red was also a common colour for women's petticoats during the Tudor period.

The long period of exceptionally cold weather that became known as the Little Ice Age was sometimes so extreme that it saw the River Thames freeze solid. To keep warm, people wore multiple layers of thermal clothing such as wools and furs. Scarlet flannel was thought to provide extra warmth and to protect from illness, as recommended in Andrew Boorde's 1542 book *A Dyetary of Helth*. The natural fibres of flannel helped to regulate temperature, and warming red was thought to ward off chills and fever, as the colour provided a psychological comfort because of its association with fire. When she was gravely ill with scarlet fever, Queen Elizabeth I wrapped herself in scarlet flannel to aid her recovery.

Even into the nineteenth century, red wool flannel continued to be a warming item. A red wool flannel redingote, or riding coat, from 1810, one of which is now in the collection of the Kyoto Costume Institute, added a protective coat over the fashionably thin muslin dresses of the time. The choice of red also tapped into the appropriation of military-wear, as the British fought in the Napoleonic wars. Red uniforms dyed with cochineal were a familiar sight in towns across the country. In *Pride and Prejudice*, Lydia is quite taken with Wickham's red uniform, with Mrs Bennet commenting: "I remember the time when I liked a red coat myself very well..."

By the late 1850s, women were increasingly taking part in genteel pursuits, and to make it easier for walking, they looped up their hems to reveal the flash of a scarlet petticoat or underskirt and colourful striped stockings. Another fashion fad in the 1860s was the red woollen "Garibaldi" bodice, named after the red shirts of the Italian revolutionary Giuseppe Garibaldi and designed in the style of a gentlemen's shirt. It was a masculine style made feminine and the precursor to the woman's blouse.

The red of lust and desire
Red has long been the colour that signifies desire, in all its illicit, lustful and romantic pleasures. Italian silk velvets often featured a pattern of red pomegranates, a popular motif during the Renaissance that symbolized fertility as well as exclusivity – because of their import costs from the Middle East, only the wealthy could afford them. Fruits were imbued with symbolism. Figs were considered

1. Carmen Kass
in Dior at the
S/S 2006 show.

2. Saoirse Ronan
as Mary Stuart
in *Mary Queen
of Scots* (2018).

erotic, because their shape and purple interior represented the vagina, and red fruits, such as cherries and strawberries, were given out as symbols of love.

While red could represent romantic desire, it also signified the deviant in its association with prostitution, stemming from the "mother of harlots". In The Book of Revelations in the Bible, the Whore of Babylon is dressed in purple and scarlet cloth, as she sits on a "scarlet coloured beast", and is "drunken with the blood of the saints, and with the blood of the martyrs of Jesus".

By the end of the Middle Ages, some towns and cities across Europe required prostitutes to wear a red piece of clothing to mark them out as sinful women, much like Hester Prynne's red letter "A" in Nathanial Hawthorne's 1850 novel The Scarlet Letter. "Her own dress was of the coarsest materials and the most sombre hue, with only that one ornament – the scarlet letter – which it was her doom to wear," he wrote.

In the cabarets of Belle Époque Paris, the wealthy and upper-crust mixed with the demi-monde to watch extravagant and racy can-can performances. The Moulin Rouge's name was suggestive of both the red light that hung outside brothels of the nineteenth century and the theatrical red curtain that was pulled back to reveal a spectacle. Henri de Toulouse-Lautrec's Au Salon de la Rue des Moulins, painted between 1894 and 1895, depicts prostitutes reclining on plush red velvet, dressed in red and pink gowns.

Translated as The Fallen Woman, Giuseppe Verdi's opera La Traviata tells the tragic story of a Parisian courtesan, Violetta, who wishes to escape her life for true love. The story, based on Alexandre Dumas's La Dame aux Camélias, inspired the plot of films like Pretty Woman (1990) and Moulin Rouge (2001). In both these movies, a red dress features significantly. Satine (Nicole Kidman) wears a red satin gown befitting her status as the most popular dancer and courtesan at the Moulin Rouge. It also symbolizes her passion, as it's worn during the musical number on top of the huge elephant in the gardens of the cabaret, when she and Ewan McGregor, as Christian, profess their love for one another.

In *Pretty Woman*, Julia Roberts wears a show-stopping red dress to the San Francisco opera to see, in a self-referential moment, *La Traviata*. The film's costume designer Marilyn Vance considered the red opera gown to be the equivalent of the "Embassy Ball" dress in 1964's *My Fair Lady*, marking one of the pinnacles of lust in the movie. But the red opera gown might have been a black ball gown if director Garry Marshall had had his way. "Garry didn't want red, he wanted black," said Vance. "I knew that it had to be red so I fought for it."

In the Metropolitan Opera's production *of La Traviata* in 2010, the red dress plays a significant role, hanging on the wall throughout the second act. It represents Violetta's life as a courtesan, and her tragic death from consumption, symbolizing the blood on her handkerchief when she coughs out her lungs.

Red continued to be used in popular culture to mark out sinfulness in women. In *Gone with the Wind*, released in 1939, the year after *Jezebel*, Scarlett O'Hara is forced by Rhett Butler to wear crimson velvet to a party, so that she can't hide her shame following her seduction of Ashley. In *Dial M for Murder* (1954), Grace Kelly's red lace gown brands her an adulterer, and also signifies how dangerous her character Margot's affair will turn out to be. The film opens with Margot in a pale pink cardigan and skirt as she sits round the breakfast table with her husband, before transitioning to embracing her lover by the fireplace, dressed in fire-engine red. "In this case, red doesn't mean stop, it means go," director Alfred Hitchcock explained.

The red smocks of the handmaids in Margaret Atwood's *The Handmaid's Tale* mark out the women who are the baby-makers in The Republic of Gilead. The red represents their fertility, as it's the colour of menstrual blood, yet it has a dual meaning – branding them as tainted women in this misogynistic society, much like the prostitutes who were forced to wear red in the Middle Ages. It also acts as a form of imprisonment – the main character Offred realizes her uniform hampers her escape and traps her, as the bright red is a beacon that marks her identity.

Red for revolution

When revolution broke out in France following the storming of the Bastille on 14 July 1789, the simple red cap worn by the working class became a patriotic symbol of overthrowing the aristocracy. The "bonnet rouge" was the cap of the sans-culottes, the most devoted followers of the revolution, who were uncompromising in their violence.

This cap was subversive in the way it referenced the outcasts of society who had been forced to wear red: slaves, convicts, prostitutes and the mentally impaired. Red had also been a marker of the aristocracy, when red heels on dark shoes were worn by select male courtiers under the reign of Louis XIV in the late seventeenth century.

During the uprising of 20 June 1792, the mob that descended on the Tuileries cornered King Louis XVI and forced the red cap on his head. The patriot newspaper *Les Revolutions de Paris* described it as "the emblem of emancipation from all servitude and the rallying sign for all enemies of despotism". After the monarchy fell in 1792, the red cap was everywhere, on pikes and flags, and as an emblem on documents. It was a particularly fitting colour to represent this bloody revolution. The red cap also became known as the Liberty Cap, after the style worn by the American revolutionaries who had inspired the people of France to rise up.

The red flag continued to fly at times of revolt in France throughout the nineteenth century, and during industrial riots, the colour red came to symbolize workers' movements as they protested for their rights. Following the Russian Revolution, the red flag was adopted for the USSR in 1922, and in 1949, it was chosen for the People's Republic of China. As the fear of communism spread in the United States in the 1940s and 1950s, the colour of the movement became a noun, marking those with communist and socialist sympathizers as "reds".

When the New York Dolls played a series of live performances in New York in 1975, after their struggles with addiction and in-fighting, they were encouraged by their new manager Malcolm McLaren to don red leather, while performing in front of a red communist flag. It was confrontational and deliberately provocative, bringing together all the symbolism of red – passion and danger, sexuality and politics.

Red by design
In referencing the red of the French revolution in his Spring/Summer 2006 collection for Dior, John Galliano created capes and coats the colour of blood clots, and emblazoned blood-splattered dresses with Marquis de Sade quotations, including "Is it not by murder that France is free today?" Red features in fashion collections as a colour that demands attention and spectacle, that can speak of both danger and desire. While Coco Chanel is strongly associated with black, she also professed to loving red, and featured it time and again as a signature colour in her collections because she saw it as forceful and lifegiving, particularly with a slash of red lipstick. "Red, it's the colour of blood and we've so much inside us it's only right to show a little outside," she once said.

"I think that a woman dressed in red is always magnificent," Italian fashion designer Valentino Garavani proclaimed. When he opened his atelier on Rome's Via Condotti, his first Spring/Summer collection in 1959 featured a vibrant poppy-red tulle cocktail dress, which he named "Fiesta". The dress was an immediate hit, launching him into rarefied fashion circles. After being championed by Jacqueline Kennedy, he became one of the most sought-after designers of the 1960s, and red played a vital role in his collections. His passion for the colour was sparked when he attended the Barcelona opera as a student, to see George Bizet's *Carmen*. "All the costumes on the stage were red," Garavani remembered. "All the women in the boxes were mostly dressed in red, and they leaned forward like geraniums on balconies, and the seats and drapes were red too ... I realized that after black and white, there was no finer colour."

There is a phenomenon known as The Red Dress Effect, where red clothing, particularly on women, elicits feelings of desire, and studies have shown that when women wear red, they attract more interest from men than those in different colours. The University of Rochester carried out psychological experiments to examine how colours enhanced women's attractiveness in the eyes of men. Those men who were shown pictures of women wearing red, or against a red background, were rated the most sexually desirable. And as reported in the International Journal of Hospitality Management, research by Nicolas Guéguen and Céline Jacob of the Université de Bretagne-Sud, France, found that waitresses who wore red lipstick achieved higher tips from male patrons.

Just as the natural world tints succulent fruit like strawberries to attract animals, humans have always used red as sexually enticing, from the deep circles of rouge on the cheeks of eighteenth-century female courtiers in France to the red lingerie promoted by companies like Victoria's Secret to spice up bedroom activities. These examples demonstrate that whether it's pillar-box or cherry, crimson or rust, red is one of the most tempestuous, powerful colours you can wear.

1

2

1. Valentino, A/W 2020/2021.

2. Nicole Kidman as Satine in *Moulin Rouge* (2001).

3. Julia Roberts
in *Pretty Woman*
(1990).

4. Valentino,
ready-to-wear
S/S 2012.

From Elsa Schiaparelli's shocking pink to
Instagram-favourite millennial pink, the colour
most associated with all things feminine has gone
through numerous identities. While it was a popular
colour for fashionable men of the eighteenth
century, when a pink silk jacket was a marker of
youthful vigour, by the 1950s, blonde bombshells
Jayne Mansfield and Marilyn Monroe helped to
reinforce pink as the colour of a traditional form of
womanhood. Pink can have a reputation as being
sickly sweet. As fashion historian Valerie Steele
says, "Some people think pink is pretty, sweet, and
romantic, others find it vulgar, silly and artificial."

Pink

Americans and Europeans may consider it the most divisive of colours, but the Japanese concept of *kawaii*, meaning "cute", fully embraces pink. Girls who follow the Lolita subculture pile on bubble-gum frills, ribbons and matching parasols, while pink Hello Kitty® accessories are much sought-after for schoolgirls and adult women alike. Pink can also be for punks. The exterior of Vivienne Westwood and Malcolm McLaren's King's Road shop spelled "SEX" in rubbery pink letters, at a time when the feminist movement had attempted to relegate pink to the historic dustbin, and the Sex Pistols and the Clash used fluorescent pink against black for their artwork as a sign of bad taste, energy and nonconformity.

While pink has a deep association with Barbie® dolls, in recent years it's been transformed into a cool, subversive fashion statement for millennials. It's beloved by a generation for whom feminism is intrinsic, where the girliness of pink has been reclaimed, and can be worn ironically, or as a confrontational declaration. And pink is not just for girls – singer Harry Styles is just one star who has ignored the gendered parameters of pink, choosing hot-pink and candy-floss suits and shirts that have earned him style icon status. As Mary Quant once said: "If you want to go unnoticed in a crowd, don't wear pink."

The creation of pink

The colour pink has long had a confused identity, where the name was most often linked with flowers. Ancient Greeks and Romans treated pink as a softer version of red, with most European languages now using a variation of the Latin *roseus*, for "rose", which traditionally defined a vibrant red. In Italy during the Renaissance, *incarnato* was used by Venetian dyers for "pink", which translated as "carnation" in English. Another carnation flower, *Dianthus plumarius*, known as "pinks" for the frilled edge of their petals (after the verb "to pink", meaning to decorate with a perforated pattern, and from which the term "pinking shears", for the scissors that create a scalloped edge, also derived) is believed to have paved the route to the English word we now use.

Pink fabrics were traditionally created by using safflower, a species of thistle originating in Asia. There are two dyes sourced from the florets: a yellow shade and a reddish one, the latter of which was used to create different salmon, blush or peach shades, and even deeper reds when combined with alkalis. Safflower was used in ancient China to dye silks in a range of pinks, while also being used to create a blusher for the cheeks. This was evident in the art of the Tang dynasty, where women were depicted wearing a variety of pink robes in works by Zhou Fang (c. 730–800 CE), including the paintings *Court Ladies Adorning Their Hair with Flowers* and *Lady with Servants.*

Venetian merchants at the beginning of the fifteenth century began importing brazilwood from India and Sumatra, and while they used the substance for red fabrics, it also created beautiful coral tones when combined with tin mordants. These new pink shades, sought-after by the rich and influential during the Renaissance, came to be considered exotic because of the far-flung origins of brazilwood.

In 1500, Portuguese explorers came across a species of tannin-rich brazilwood on the South American coast that created stronger, longer-lasting shades of red and pink from its pigment, *brazilin*. Upon the pigment's discovery, the heartwood of these trees was in high demand for its properties as a dye. Such was its value it would be the source for the name of this new land: Brazil. As the Portuguese held a monopoly over brazilwood, other countries like France tried to get their own foothold in South America to access the dyestuff, and Portuguese ships were regularly targeted by pirates for their bounty. This precious commodity also further encouraged a fashion for pink across Europe, and by the mid-1700s, European society championed the colour as a symbol of exoticism and luxury. Names like "China pink", "Persian pink" and "Congo pink" further highlighted the colour's supposedly "foreign" appeal. In 1956, photographer Norman Parkinson travelled on assignment for British *Vogue* to Jaipur, known as the Pink City of Rajasthan, where he photographed model Anne Gunning in a pink mohair coat next to an elaborately decorated elephant and local men in fuchsia tunics and turbans. While the images could now be considered cultural appropriation of a former colony, Diana Vreeland, formidable editor of *Harper's Bazaar*, and later *Vogue*, adored pink, and on their publication she heralded these photos for their vivid depictions of the culture and colours of India, saying "How clever of you, Mr Parkinson, to know that pink is the navy blue of India."

Jaipur is known as the Pink City, and as well as the royal palace being built with pink and red sandstone, Maharaja Sawai Ram Singh II ordered every building to be spruced up with pink paint, the colour of hospitality, to welcome Albert Edward, the Prince of Wales, on his state visit in 1876. Fuchsia pink saris and tunics were popular in the city, and throughout Rajasthan, matching the pink rose petals for sale in the markets. Prior to the nineteenth century, Indian dyers were some of the most advanced in their knowledge of natural dyes and mordants, particularly when it came to achieving pinks and reds with safflower and lac, the resin from tiny insects that gather on fig trees.

William Perkin's discovery of the synthetic dye mauveine in 1856 led to the popularity of brilliant aniline dyes like fuchsine, which was first discovered by August Wilhelm von Hofmann in 1858, and magenta, a purple-pink tone patented by François-Emmanuel Verguin in 1859, which was also referred to as "Solferino". In July 1860, *The Englishwoman's Domestic Magazine* heralded for evening dresses "the new shades of pink, called Solferino and Magenta".

1. Christian Berard illustration of a dress by Elsa Schiaparelli, from *Vogue*, 1937.

2. *The Swing* (c.1767) by Jean-Honoré Fragonard.

3. Marilyn Monroe in *Gentlemen Prefer Blondes* (1953).

As brilliant pink was becoming increasingly democratic and accessible, worn among the servant classes and as a colour for men's socks, it began to be considered "vulgar" and in "bad taste" for women's fashions. The fuchsine dye used for socks reacted with sweat from the skin, causing painful inflammation of the feet, and by the end of the nineteenth century, as more reports of the toxicity of the dye were revealed, brilliant pinks had gained negative associations.

Rococo pink

As France became the dominant power in Europe in the eighteenth century, fashions shifted from the black of the Spanish courts to the lighter hues of the Enlightenment period. Rococo paintings by artists like François Boucher and Jean-Honoré Fragonard created a sense of playfulness and fantasy with their rosy-cheeked cherubs and women courtiers in peach and strawberry silk gowns, surrounded by nature.

The popularity of pink was enhanced by the discovery of the South American species of brazilwood, which created a brighter, long-lasting pink. Madame de Pompadour, mistress of King Louis XV, was the most influential woman of the time, and such was her love of pink that, in 1757, a French chemist called Jean Hellot named a shade pink after her: Pompadour pink. Boucher's 1750 portrait, *Madame de Pompadour at Her Toilette*, shows the courtesan applying pink blush to her cheeks, which alluringly matches the pink touches on her gown. Not only does it make her a vision of youthful beauty, but the colour, achieved by blending cochineal with white ochre, possessed an erotic charge in its resemblance to the sensual parts of the body, such as flesh, lips and nipples. Pale pink was considered particularly erotic for lingerie, as it blended with Caucasian flesh tones at a time when the fashion was for pale skin with a slight touch of pink. Émile

Zola, in his novel *Au Bonheur des Dames* (1883), wrote of the lingerie in a department store: "as if a group of pretty girls had undressed, piece by piece, down to the satin nudity of their skin".

According to A. Cassandra Albinson, in her essay "Feminine desire and fragility: pink in eighteenth-century portraiture", women in betrothal portraits in the sixteenth and seventeenth centuries often held a carnation to represent their sexual reproduction, symbolizing that, like the pink flower in their hand, they were at their sexual peak. With pink representing a woman at her most fertile, it was therefore thought unsuitable for those over 30 – at the time considered middle age – as were other youthful adornments, such as feathers and flowers. Salon hostess Madame Necker once commented: "When we see a pink gown, we expect to see a pretty face next; and if the woman who wears the garment is no longer young, we are unpleasantly surprised." This view was made clear in the satirical 1743 pastel *Folly Embellishing Old Age with the Adornments of Youth* by Charles-Antoine Coypel, depicting an elderly woman being attended at her vanity desk, considered ridiculously dressed in pale pink. Expressions such as "in the pink" also implied it was a colour reserved for youth, regardless of whether that was for men or women.

Think pink
The notion of pink as a fresh, feminine colour gained ground in the twentieth century. In 1936, Italian fashion designer Elsa Schiaparelli was inspired by the dimensions of the actress Mae West's figure to create a new perfume bottle in the shape of a woman's body. She wanted the name to begin with an S, to be an alliteration of her name, and when it came to choosing the colour for the bottle, she described in her memoirs how:

[It] flashed in front of my eyes. Bright, impossible, impudent, becoming, life-giving, like all the light and the birds and the fish in the world put together, a colour of China and Peru but not of the West – a shocking colour, pure and undiluted. So I called the perfume "Shocking" ... The success was immense and immediate. The perfume, without advertising of any sort, took a leading place, and the colour "shocking" established itself for ever as a classic.

The colour of the perfume bottle launched an eye-catching shade of pink, known as shocking pink, which she also used for her fashion line, including for a brilliant satin cape with a sun emblazoned on the back. Schiaparelli teamed up with surrealist artist Salvador Dalí, who used both shocking pink and red for a series of sofas inspired by Mae West's lips in 1936. Dalí and Schiaparelli also collaborated on a black avant-garde hat in the shape of an upside-down shoe, with a shocking-pink velvet heel. Daisy Fellowes, one of the most fashionable and scandalous women of the time, was one of the few women fearless enough to wear it.

In the years after the Second World War, women were encouraged to play the perfect housewife, to ensure that men didn't feel like their traditional roles had been usurped while they'd been overseas fighting. After having donned khaki and navy-blue uniforms to do their part in the war effort, women's fashions in the post-war period were bursting with colour, particularly pink.

Christian Dior made waves with his debut collection in 1947, dubbed the New Look because it was the antithesis of the utilitarian silhouette – and the clothes and textiles rationing – of the war years. In some ways, it was regressive in how it created an idealized version of a woman's body through padding and corseting. His gowns and suits used swathes of luxury fabric, and having been inspired by the petals of roses, he naturally adopted pink for his collections, including his Venus ball gown from the Autumn/Winter 1949–50 collection, which was a fantasy of pale pink silk tulle covered in glittering petals.

The 1950s in America was a time of great prosperity as consumerism rocketed, and pink products were much more visible in magazine adverts and in department stores. As Lynn Peril writes in her book *Pink Think*, "Americans were in the throes of what can only be described as pinkmania."

There were pink fashions, Playtex underwear in "pink-ice", and a huge range of pink shades for matching lips and nails. In an advert for Revlon in 1959, the copy celebrates "a new ... hot ... vibrant pink-fashion elegance from Italy! Pink that tingles with life and color ... so wildly ... wilfully ... wonderfully pink." An article in the *New York Times* in April 1959 discussed Elizabeth Arden's new shade of "Arden pink" for her lipstick and clothing lines. In the article she described how "pink is for all women, not just bon-bon blondes" and that there were "cocktail and dinner" dresses in Arden pink. But it went even further than make-up and clothing. "Women who want pink to go to their heads" could try a new pink rinse that "gives the hair a very soft, low-keyed pink highlight".

In the movie *Funny Face* (1957), starring Audrey Hepburn and Fred Astaire, the musical number 'Think Pink' played up the power of fashion magazines as editor Maggie Prescott (Kay Thompson) promotes pink as the hot new colour, saying: "Banish the black! Burn the blue! And bury the beige!" When Prescott is asked if she'll wear pink too, she replies sharply, "I wouldn't be caught dead!"

Maggie is the older, cynical career woman who is portrayed as unlikely to ever get married, and therefore has no desire to wear pink to help attract a man and capture a future husband, as she is insinuating of her younger readers. In this early Cold War period, where conservative values were dominant, women were constantly told – in Hollywood movies, commercials and magazine editorials – that their role was to be feminine, soft and charming so that they could fulfil their duties as a wife and mother. In her 2002 book, Peril described "pink think" as a set of ideas and attitudes about the correct behaviour for females, saying it was:

... a groupthink that was consciously or not adhered to by advice writers, manufacturers of toys and other consumer products, experts in many walks of life, and the public at large, particularly during the years spanning the mid-twentieth century ... this mythical standard, which suggests that women and girls are always gentle, soft, delicate, nurturing beings made of "sugar and spice and everything nice".

Penny Sparke, in her 1995 book *As Long as It's Pink: The Sexual Politics of Taste*, writes that pink "represented the emphasis on distinctive gendering that underpinned 1950s society, ensuring that women were women and men were men. Gendering had to start at an early age, and parents were the key role models. The use of pink in the home emphasized the essential femininity of girls and women."

Reinforcing this idea of traditional roles was First Lady Mamie Eisenhower, wife of President Dwight D. "Ike" Eisenhower. She spent years as an army wife travelling the world with Ike the general, acting as the perfect smiling hostess who took pride in husband and home, and was fond of reinforcing this with statements like, "Ike runs the country. I turn the pork chops!"

She was also a lover of all things pink. For her husband's inaugural ball in 1953, she captured the public's imagination with a candy-floss pink gown, designed by Nettie Rosenstein, sparkling with over 2,000 pink rhinestones. After moving into the White House, she ensured her private rooms, including her bathroom, were decorated in a specific shade of pink which became known as Mamie pink or First Lady pink. It was the same pink she had decorated her homes when living abroad with Ike. The First Lady's love of pink led to a boom in pink across America, not only for pink cocktail gowns but also for bathrooms and even for kitchens, where housewives whipped up batches of her recipe for million-dollar fudge.

Pink was also embraced by starlet Jayne Mansfield, as a way of reinforcing her own brand of ditzy femininity. If the idealized feminine form in the 1950s was blonde and voluptuous, starlet Mansfield epitomized the stereotype. In addition to driving a pink Jaguar, she was married in a skin-tight pink lace gown. Her Sunset Boulevard home was called the "Pink Palace", and on one occasion, her new pink swimming pool was filled to the brim with pink champagne. "Men want women to be pink, helpless and do a lot of deep breathing," she said. However, she later reflected that her embracing of pink was an attention-craving publicity opportunity. "Pink was my color, because it made me happy ... Now I had something to intrigue the photographers. Come up for a drink and paint me pink. I'd invite anyone who had a camera. I'd add I would be happy to pose for any layouts they'd like. I was desperate."

Hollywood movies in the 1950s adopted pink as a girlish, fun colour which not only popped on screen as many movies embraced Technicolor, but also served to reinforce the traditional gender roles that were being promoted in society, along with a conservative outlook. Marilyn Monroe was the ultimate pin-up of the 1950s, and her performance of 'Diamonds Are a Girl's Best Friend' in *Gentlemen Prefer Blondes* (1953) played up to the notions of both consumerism and femininity that marked the era. The burlesque-inspired costumes for the movie's two stars, Jane Russell and Marilyn Monroe, were designed by William

Travilla to enhance the decade's notion of womanhood. But he found he was under particular pressure from the censorship office, headed by Joseph Breen, to ensure costumes wouldn't contravene the strict moral codes that controlled Hollywood's output by revealing too much thigh, cleavage or belly button. Many of Travilla's costumes for Monroe were rejected as they were "deliberately designed to attract vulgar attention to her breasts", as outlined in Production Code records from November 1952.

While the film was in production, images of Monroe from a nude photoshoot before she was famous were bought and published by *Playboy* magazine, and the studio, Twentieth Century Fox, was worried that the scandal of the photos would have repercussions for Monroe's reputation. For the 'Diamonds Are a Girl's Best Friend' number, Travilla had initially designed a sheer black body stocking with strategically placed rhinestones, but in the wake of the nude photos, studio boss Darryl Zanuck sent Travilla a memo – "cover her up" – and he was forced to come up with a new concept. He wrapped her in stiff pink taffeta to create the now-iconic strapless gown, which featured a big bow at the back, and was worn with matching opera gloves. In Technicolor, the pale pink showed up bolder and brighter against the pink set design, and reaffirmed pink as the feminine colour of the 1950s.

Pink for girls

Prior to the twentieth century, infants had worn simple white gowns for practical reasons – they were cheap, and could easily be boiled and bleached. Gender-coding of pink and blue didn't become popular until the post-Second World War baby boom.

In *Little Women*, Louisa May Alcott writes, "Amy put a blue ribbon on the boy and a pink on the girl, French fashion, so you can always tell." This suggests that the classification of pink for girls was a French innovation, yet the origins are unclear. By 1890, this concept still hadn't travelled across the Atlantic. That year, *Ladies' Home Journal* noted: "Pure white is used for all babies. Blue is for girls and pink is for boys, when a color is wished." Similarly, in an article on baby clothes in the *New York Times* in July 1893, readers were advised to "always give pink to a boy and blue to a girl" because "the boy's outlook is so much more roseate than the girl's ... that it is enough to make a girl baby blue to think of living a woman's life in the world."

In her 2012 study of the clothing of children in the United States up to the age of about six or seven, Jo B. Paoletti identified when girls were assigned pink, and boys were assigned blue. She noted that Sigmund Freud introduced the idea that very early experiences unconsciously shape our adult natures, particularly our sexual desires. With the publication of further psychological studies on the subject of sexual identity in child development, this led to the belief that a child's gender should be reinforced as early as possible.

By the late 1940s, feminine details were purged from the clothing of little boys, particularly pink. This was because there was a belief that masculinity in baby boys should be protected and reinforced to ensure they were not harmed by being mistaken for a girl, which, so the thinking went, would lead to "dangerous" homosexuality. In 1941, Dr Leslie B. Hohman wrote of the dangers of "Girlish Boys and Boyish Girls", as his article was entitled, in *Ladies' Home Journal*. He gave the example of a 12-year-old boy whose mother was concerned he was displaying too much "girlishness". Hohman sent the boy to military school to retrain him as "a normal manly youth". Blamed for this excessive femininity was his mother's "admiring notice at eighteen months when he stroked with apparent delight a pink satin dress she wore".

Similarly, girls were given pink to ensure they were sufficiently feminine, in order to fulfil their own roles as wives and mothers. Second-wave feminists in the 1970s targeted pink as a colour that pigeonholed girls and stymied their potential, and instead promoted unisex clothing for children, in gender-neutral green and orange. However, this push for unisex colours inevitably led to a backlash.

During the 1980s, pink was reinforced as very much a girls' colour, for both clothing and toys, and this was enhanced by new prenatal technologies. Ultrasounds revealed to parents the sex of their child during pregnancy, and they could therefore shop for, and be gifted, the appropriate colour of products for their baby before its birth.

By the early 2000s, pink was ubiquitous for girls and women in every product available – from running shoes and tracksuits to bubblegum-pink Motorola flip phones. In comparison to the "ladette" culture of the 1990s, and the feminist punk bands like Bikini Kill and Courtney Love's Hole, the 2000s saw pop music reinvigorated by stars like Britney Spears and Christina Aguilera, who simultaneously appealed to little girls and young women by playing up to precocious notions of femininity. New cultural icons like Paris Hilton were regularly snapped by paparazzi in pink Juicy Couture tracksuits, while Victoria's Secret marketed pink underwear as worn by their supermodel Angels. Pink became hyper-sexualized, with a trend for pink accessories from the Playboy brand, such as T-shirts, pencil cases and purses, inappropriately targeted at pre-teen girls.

Pink was further promoted in the film *Legally Blonde* (2001), by the character Elle Woods, played by Reese Witherspoon, who considers pink her signature colour. With her ditzy airhead demeanour and her fashion choices, it's assumed she lacks intelligence. After successfully passing the entrance exam and gaining admission, she arrives at Harvard Law School in a pink convertible and dressed in a tight pink leather suit – to much ridicule. "Check out Malibu Barbie," says one heckler. "Where's the beach, honey?" When her classmates trick her into wearing a fancy-dress costume to a party, she arrives in her candy-floss pink Playboy bunny suit, and her ex-boyfriend Warner simultaneously tries to come onto her while telling her, "You're not smart enough, sweetie" to study at law school. Woods is constantly infantilized by her love of pink, yet she manages to disprove her critics while continuing to unashamedly embrace her favourite colour.

The film *Mean Girls* (2004) played up to the teenage post-feminist love of pink, when the group of popular girls known as the Plastics wear pink every Wednesday. Costume designer Mary Jane Fort wanted the bitchy girls to look sugary sweet. "When you see this group, you want to feel like you walked into something delicious even though it's kind of bad for you," she said.

This pink culture of the new millennium was further adopted for Sofia Coppola's *Marie Antoinette* (2006), which was a punk and sugar-bombed take on the life of the French queen, played by Kirsten Dunst, viewed through a post-feminist lens. In their essay "*Marie Antoinette*: Fashion, Third-Wave Feminism and Chick Culture", Suzanne Ferriss and Mallory Young argued that Coppola's film represented the contemporary "chick culture" of third wave feminism, using costume to help audiences identify with her journey, as a celebrity teen queen in the realm of Paris Hilton, Elle Woods in *Legally Blonde*, or Dunst herself. Coppola's films have often celebrated unashamed girl-culture, with her use of pink also incorporated into *Lost in Translation* (2003), with the close-up of pink knickers on Scarlett Johansson in the opening moments, and the trend-setting pink wig worn by her during the karaoke scene.

The film's title sequence, with *Marie Antoinette* printed in pink and black, borrowed from the aesthetic of punk bands, which also inspired the modern soundtrack, and Coppola gave the film's costume designer, Milena Canonero, a box of pastel Ladurée macarons as a

1. Kirsten Dunst as Marie Antoinette in Sofia Coppola's 2006 film.

2. Jodie Comer as Villanelle in *Killing Eve*.

1. Rihanna's Fenty x Puma collection at Paris Fashion Week S/S 2017.

2. Gucci, F/W 2016/17, Milan Fashion Week

3. Viktor&Rolf, haute couture S/S 2019.

reference for the wardrobe confections, which made frequent use of pink for dresses, ribbons, shoes and fans. In one shot from the film, the queen reclines on a chaise longue, surrounding by sumptuous pink iced cakes and tarts, as a lady-in-waiting slips a pink shoe onto her foot. The aesthetics of the film make life at Versailles appear deliciously luxurious – an extravagant lifestyle that ultimately leads to the downfall of the royal family.

Millennial pink

Oksana Astankova, aka the fictional character Villanelle, became a fashion sensation following the release of the television series *Killing Eve* in 2018. Despite being a psychopathic assassin with ever-inventive ways of dispatching her targets, the character, played by Jodie Comer, set trends with her impeccable style. One of the pieces that gained the most attention was a pink tulle dress by designer Molly Goddard that launched fan accounts and Reddit threads. The pink was used ironically – that a woman so cold-blooded could wear a colour that is supposed to be soft and feminine. The dress is also reminiscent of the tulle ballet dresses beloved by little girls, in the pale pink that has been linked with ballerinas ever since Marie Taglioni wore pink tights for *La Sylphide* in 1832.

A similarly ironic take was Viktor&Rolf's candy-pink 2019 creation, made from layers of pink tulle. It was inspired by the excesses of Marie Antoinette, with the words *Less is More* in bold print – reflecting the online meme culture of creating hashtags and slogans. The colour perfectly encapsulated the adoption of pink by the Instagram generation as part of a wider trend for all things kitsch, such as flamingos, watermelons and lobsters. Flamingos were ubiquitous in 2017, appearing as plastic garden ornaments, inflatable pool toys (inspired by Taylor Swift's 2015 Fourth of July pool party) and as a print on Marc Jacobs's Spring 2015 collection, followed by Gucci, with pink flamingos in their pre-Fall 2016 campaign and Prada, with their flamingo-themed perfume. The flamingo harked back to 1950s aesthetics, of Miami Beach and Elvis's musical film *Blue Hawaii* (1961), and of the Beverly Hills Hotel, known as the Pink Palace – a vestige of tropical kitsch.

When Rihanna launched her Fenty x Puma Spring/Summer 2017 collection during Paris Fashion Week, she embraced a gender-fluid style of beige-pink tracksuits and pale-pink trainers with soft satin bows, like those of a ballet slipper, which tapped into a wider trend for a shade known as "millennial pink". Closer to salmon than the bubblegum pink of the *Killing Eve* dress, it was a shade that was wearable, adaptable and particularly looked good as a backdrop for lush green plants and cacti.

The phenomenon of millennial pink was identified by Veronique Hyland's article in August 2016, "Why Is Millennial Pink Suddenly So Popular?", which appeared in *New York* magazine. "Remember when pink was déclassé?" Hyland wrote. She explained:

> Pink used to be Malibu Barbie® and Bubble Yum and all the bright plastic items that many of us in this particular group were steered away from as kids. And that specific shade of pink is not the one that's resurfaced. Instead it's ironic pink, pink without the sugary prettiness. It's a non-color that doesn't commit, whose semi-ugliness is proof of its sophistication.

Pink for men

By the 1960s, as the feminist movement gained pace and toxic masculinity escalated as male identity felt threatened, pink largely disappeared from men's wardrobes, and had for some time been considered inappropriate when worn by little boys. By the 1980s, pink was so strongly associated with femininity that a man who wore pink was considered eccentric.

1. Harry Styles in an Edward Sexton suit on *Today*, 2017.

2. Sugar Ray Robinson with his pink Cadillac in Harlem, 1950s.

In the mid 1990s, at the infamous correctional facility run by Sheriff Joe Arpaio in Maricopa County, Arizona, the male inmates were given pink underpants, sandals and towels. This was ostensibly a way to keep the inmates from taking the garments with them upon their release from prison. The pink was chosen in order to shame the men, as it was considered to be emasculating. This idea harked back to Nazi Germany, when men who were imprisoned for being homosexual were forced to wear a pink triangle, possibly linked to the term *Rosarote*, which was used for male sex workers in Germany, and translates as pink-red. In 1987, the AIDS Coalition to Unleash Power (ACT UP) adopted a pink triangle as their logo, reclaiming the symbol as empowering rather than oppressive.

While pink had been popular for men in the eighteenth century, in the Industrial Age men were given a uniform of dark suits, and it was considered rather foppish to wear too much colour or decoration. In the 1920s, when a dandy style was promoted by leading figures like the Prince of Wales, pink shirts or suits were sometimes worn by some men, but it was a symbol of one who tried too hard to be fashionable. In the novel *The Great Gatsby* (1925), Jay Gatsby wears a pink suit, which sparks Tom Buchanan's incredulity that Gatsby went to Oxford. Buchanan sees the colour as being socially inferior – "An Oxford man! ... Like hell he is! He wears a pink suit." Pink shirts were, however, being marketed by Brooks Brothers from the 1920s onwards, which spoke to an Ivy League sense of style, of vacations in Palm Beach – and the knowledge that for those with money and power, rules can be broken. This trend reached new heights in the 1950s with shoes, jackets and socks also being made available in various shades of pink, for those who dared to wear them. Elvis Presley made stage appearances in pink trousers and a black jacket, or in pink jumpsuits covered in rhinestones.

In the 1950s, he bought a pink Cadillac, just like one owned by Sugar Ray Robinson. The boxer said he fell in love with pink on his visit to Miami, where the art deco buildings are painted in pastels, and when he brought it back to Harlem, he recounted that everyone there saw it as the "'Hope Diamond' of the American Dream".

This was a moment of mainstream non-conformity that was over within the decade. Author Karal Ann Marling suggests that this short-lived masculine embrace of pink was merely "part of the general fascination with chromatic variety" of the time, tapping into the fever for consumerism.

Pink now

The rules of pink for men have long been ignored by certain subcultures. In the side-by-side capitals of the Republic of Congo and the Democratic Republic of Congo – respectively, Brazzaville and Kinshasa – pink is embraced by the dandyish followers of La Sape, which stands for Société des Ambianceurs et des Personnes Élégantes (the Society of Tastemakers and Elegant People). These working-class men, known as sapeurs, have grown up in countries torn apart by civil war, and to express their identities they embrace the elegance of French colonial style in a range of bright colours. In a 2011 *Wall Street Journal* profile, journalist Tom Downey described Hassan Salvador's "salmon-colored silk scarf" worn with a sport coat, despite the 90-degree heat of Brazzaville, while the cover of photographer Daniele Tamagni's 2009 book *Gentlemen of the Bacongo* featured a sapeur strutting in a candy-floss pink suit, with a cerise tie, brogues and red bowler hat.

The world of hip-hop also has its proponents of pink. In 2002, Harlem rapper Cam'ron attended New York Fashion Week in a pink mink coat and hat, and was credited with driving the popularity of pink in the genre.

It was a way of showing confidence in his own masculinity, and that he rejected the stereotypes around pink. Similarly fashion-forward artists like Frank Ocean, with his dyed pink hair in 2017, wear the colour to show they aren't afraid of defying expectations. Singer Harry Styles is also a frequent wearer of the colour, choosing a pink satin shirt with white trousers for the cover of his debut album, and a pink suit with black shirt by British designer Edward Sexton when performing on *Today* in 2017. The suit, cut in a 1970s style, deliberately referenced a pink suit worn by Mick Jagger in 1970. When Styles graced the cover of *Rolling Stone* magazine's May 2017 issue, dressed in a pink satin shirt with pussy bow by Alexander McQueen, he quoted the Clash's Paul Simonon in saying, "Pink is the only true rock & roll colour." Following in the footsteps of 1970s male peacocks such as Jagger and David Bowie, Styles has made the colour his own, ignoring the gendered rules of pink that society has internalized.

In contrast, Singer Janelle Monáe pushed the notion of "pink for girls" further in her 2018 single 'PYNK', which was a tribute to the vagina, and in the music video, where she and her dancers wore labia-shaped pink pants designed by Duran Lantink.

From its early depictions in Tang dynasty art and rococo art, pink has played on notions of femininity, youthfulness, fertility and the erotic, even if the concept of pink for a girl wasn't firmly established until the 1960s. Because of these feminine associations, pink is also a powerful colour for raising awareness of breast cancer and women's rights – from the pink saris worn by a female vigilante group, the Gulabi (pink) Gang, who fight for injustice against women, to the pink pussy hats worn at the Women's March of January 2017. Pink may be feminine, but that doesn't diminish its power.

1. Model Winnie Harlow at the 2019 Vanity Fair Oscar Party.

2. Carolina Herrera, ready-to-wear F/W 2019, New York Fashion Week.

3. Sapeurs in Kinshasa, Democratic Republic of Congo, 2012.

When news broke around the world in 1995 that Hugh Grant had solicited a prostitute on Hollywood Boulevard, his girlfriend Elizabeth Hurley was immediately mobbed by paparazzi. Greeted by a throng of photographers on her doorstep, she did not look aggrieved, but dazzled in white jeans, white strappy sandals, a silver top, and dark shades. Pristine white not only helped her keep cool with the world's spotlight on her and the revelation that her long-term partner had cheated, but the look underpinned the notion of Hurley as a confident, high-maintenance woman who could pull off one of the trickiest colours for jeans. Over the years since, the white jean has been a staple of her wardrobe, with the model and actress once noting that she owned around 50 pairs.

White

Jess Cartney-Morley, writing in the *Guardian* in June 2015 to celebrate Liz Hurley's 50th birthday, noted that white jeans are the "perfect off-duty wear for a woman who doesn't really do dressing down, [and] project money, frivolity and – thanks to that Jilly Cooper-ish jodhpur tightness – a certain frolickiness. Still the uniform of women who drink white wine on King's Road, Chelsea."

White jeans are a high-maintenance garment, as a tiny spot of dirt will immediately stand out, and so they project an image of wealth and luxury, for wearing on expensive yachting holidays on the Mediterranean, or for relaxing at a member's club. Spotless white clothing was traditionally worn only by those who could afford it – those who didn't concern themselves with dirtying their clothes through manual labour, and since the nineteenth century, cool-white linen suits and dresses were the vacationing wardrobe of choice for the leisured classes.

There's also a sensuality to wearing white, projecting a contradiction between innocence and abandon, as used to great effect by Marilyn Monroe when cocooned in her favourite white towelling robes. In the film *Cat on a Hot Tin Roof* (1958), Elizabeth Taylor's white Grecian-style chiffon gown, designed by Helen Rose and later nicknamed "The Cat" dress, softens the hard, fiery character of Maggie the Cat, making her seem softer and kittenish.

While white conveys indulgence, it can also be considered tacky if worn in the wrong way. In the 1980s, there were countless jokes about Essex girls wearing white stilettos, and in America, there's a social convention that white shouldn't be worn after Labor Day, as grotesquely parodied in John Waters's 1994 film *Serial Mom*. After the Labor Day holiday was introduced in 1894, the first Monday of September marked the time that light summer clothing was expected to be packed away for fall to return to the sober clothing of business and college.

For Coco Chanel, white not only meant luxury – she wore her white satin pyjamas on the Venice Lido – but also represented purity and cleanliness. It reminded her of the freshly laundered sheets and white petticoats at the convent where she was raised, as for centuries white linen was used for undergarments, to allow the body to keep cool and to protect the outer clothing from dirt.

In cultural traditions around the world, white represents purity and virginity. In ancient Rome, the priestesses of Vesta wore white linen robes as a symbol of chastity, and in Islamic countries, plain white cotton is worn as a sign of devotion, as expensive silks were only for wearing in paradise. White is the colour of freshly fallen snow, of milk and of vanilla ice cream – all of which imply a degree of simplicity and innocence. White light reflects back all the colours of the spectrum, and so a white object becomes a blank canvas on which all other colours could be displayed.

The story of white linen

Linen made from flax is one of the earliest textiles to have been discovered; there is evidence of it being woven in ancient Egypt from around 5000 BC. The Egyptians developed their own industry upon the cultivation of flax, wherein the stem was used to make baskets, the seeds for producing linseed oil and the fibres for spinning into white linen, the universal textile for clothing people of all status. They used basic loom-length pieces of white cloth to form dresses, loincloths and cloaks, and there were five different grades of linen, with the finest of linen reserved for royals, and referred to as "woven moonlight".

Fine white linen for the Egyptians was a symbol of light and purity, and played an important role in burial traditions. Swathes of linen were wrapped tightly around mummies and on statues, examples of which were discovered by archaeologist Howard Carter in 1922 in

King Tutankhamun's tomb. In the UCL Petrie Museum of Egyptian Archaeology in London, there are two floor-length, figure-hugging white linen dresses, dating from 2500 BCE, which were discovered in the "Extinct city" of Deshasheh in 1897, and are believed to have been used as funerary goods.

By the Middle Ages, when linen was in high demand across Europe, the highest-quality linen was known as "Holland", after the country it came from. The Dutch producers dominated the trade with a secret method that involved soaking the fabric in lye and sour milk for weeks at a time, and then leaving the fabric to bleach in the sun. It was a time-consuming process which could take up to eight months and would require the use of vast fields for laying out the fabric to soak up the sun's rays.

Linen played an important role in keeping the body clean at a time when soap was a rare luxury item. Wool and silk could not be washed in water without being damaged, so washable white linen undergarments acted as a second skin to protect the more expensive outer garments from the body's secretions. The Tudors believed that the best way to keep clean was to frequently change into freshly laundered linen shirts, chemises, hose and caps, as these absorbed sweat, helped the body to keep cool and protected the skin from rougher outer garments.

As the Virgin Queen, Elizabeth I chose to enhance her divine image by wearing expensive white silk gowns and adorning herself with gleaming white pearls. A visitor to the late Tudor court noted how Elizabeth was dressed in white silk and pearls and that "the Ladies of the Court followed next to her, very handsome and well-shaped, and for the most part dressed in white."

In the striking portrait of Elizabeth I by Marcus Gheeraerts the Younger, painted around 1592 and known as the "Ditchley portrait", the queen wears an enormous white gown with huge sleeves and a hooped petticoat

1. *The Graces in a High Wind* (1810), James Gillray.

2. *Marie Antoinette in a Chemise Dress* (1783), Elisabeth Louise Vigée Le Brun.

3. Elizabeth Hurley, 1995.

known as a farthingale, a cloak and an excessive lace collar, giving her the appearance of a frilled lizard. Everything about the dress is excessive, and the white silk satin studded with jewels and pearls denotes her purity. Even her skin is as white as can be, achieved through the use of a lead paste called "Venetian ceruse". An exaggerated white skin was considered desirable because it differentiated between the leisured classes and those who worked outside – however, it was incredibly toxic, leading to skin damage, lead poisoning and hair loss.

Queen Elizabeth I was famed for her dramatic frilled ruffs, which she wore to help her dominate the room, and with her influence, starched linen ruffs became the only fashion to wear in court.

The whimsy of white muslin

In the eighteenth century, France was the fashion centre of the world, and Marie Antoinette was the ruler – and what she wore sent aristocrats into a frenzy, whether it was for a flurry of feathers on the poufs that rested on her towering powdered wigs, or the hot new colour for silk for the *robe à la française*. In 1775, with reports that the queen was wearing a gown in an ash-grey colour dubbed "queen's hair" at Fontainebleau, courtiers immediately dispatched their servants to buy up fabrics in this shade. When her first son, Louis Joseph, was born in 1781, an olive-brown shade, known as *"caca dauphin"*, was created in honour of the contents of the young dauphin's nappies.

The queen was frivolous and immature in her constant desire for praise, and because all the trimmings, accessories and colours in her wardrobe were intensely scrutinized and splashed across the new fashion magazines, which first appeared in 1770, she spent lavishly. In 1785, Marie Antoinette frittered over 258,00 livres on her wardrobe – more than twice her annual budget – leading to her unflattering nickname "Madame Déficit".

One of the queen's passions was her informal gardens at the small palace, or the Petit Trianon, on the grounds of Versailles. She considered it a romantic countryside retreat where she could truly be herself. She asked her couturier Rose Bertin to provide her with whimsical, pastoral, white muslin chemises inspired by Jean-Jacques Rousseau's writings and rococo paintings, by artists like François Boucher, that romanticized nature.

Known as a "*chemise à la reine*", after both the influential queen and the linen shifts worn under clothing, it was pulled on over the head and fitted to the body with drawstrings. Featuring flounces around the neck and at the hem, and constructed from light fabrics like muslin, gauze, lawn, and linen, the chemise offered a freedom of movement that was a major shift from the court fashion of previous decades for elaborate trains and wigs, and wide panniers that could barely be squeezed through doorways.

In 1783, the court painter Élisabeth Louise Vigée Le Brun caused a scandal when her portrait of the queen in her white chemise and straw hat was put on display at the prestigious Salon exhibition. The dress was considered so informal that it led to rumours that the queen had been painted in her underwear.

This romanticizing of peasant life by someone considered so frivolous and unbridled in her spending as Marie Antoinette was an insult to the real misery and suffering of the poor across France. By setting a trend for imported muslin, she was also denounced by the Lyon silk industry for ruining their trade; just one of the ways the queen began to be despised by her citizens. With rumours of her excesses and extravagances, her gambling and the flippant remarks she was rumoured to have uttered, such as "Let them eat cake", she was hissed at when attending the opera and lambasted in the press. This hatred and resentment would eventually spark the revolution in 1789, when the royal family were imprisoned in Paris and both she and husband Louis XVI would face the guillotine. On the day of her execution, a year after her husband was killed, Marie Antoinette was led to the scaffold in a simple white dress and linen cap, much like the chemises she had favoured in the years before. The white she wore was also symbolic of her role as royal widow, as it was traditionally the colour worn by widowed queens in France, and was known as *le deuil blanc*, translated as "white mourning". In the last five years of her life, Marie Antoinette was almost always in mourning, with the death of two children and the loss of close family members, and this is another explanation as to why she so often wore white.

Marie Antoinette may have been ridiculed for her simple white dresses when she dressed up as a milkmaid, but following the French Revolution, white came to denote freedom and liberty during the Directoire period. The leaders of the new regime took pride in looking dishevelled, with any man who appeared in a clean shirt being deemed a "fop". At the same time, the overwhelming fashion for women in Paris was for sheer, high-waisted white gowns and flat shoes, which paid tribute to the ancient statues of the Greek and Roman republics. Their muslin gowns were so sheer that they gave the wearer the appearance of being in a state of undress, and led to rumours that women in Paris were practically naked.

For those who wanted to show their secret support for the royals while also following the rules of the republic, white was coded, as it was both the colour of the Republic and of the Bourbon royals. A rebellious group of aristocratic women, known as the *Merveilleuses*, were particularly shocking in their transparent neoclassical white gowns, which were often called "woven air". Julie Adélaïde Récamier and Thérésa Tallien were notable *Merveilleuses* who held popular salons, and were captured in paintings dressed in sheer white gowns with plunging necklines.

Ava Gardner in a publicity shot for *One Touch of Venus* (1948).

White in the age of Austen

When Fanny Price in Jane Austen's *Mansfield Park* (1814) worries she is overdressed at a dinner party, wearing a white gown that she had bought to wear at her cousin's wedding, she is told by her cousin Edmund, whom she will later marry, "A woman can never be too fine while she is all in white. No, I see no finery about you; nothing but what is perfectly proper."

White gowns featured frequently in the works of Jane Austen, reflecting the neoclassical fashions of the Regency period in Britain from 1790 to 1820. Mrs Allen tells Catherine Morland in *Northanger Abbey* (1817) that when she visits Eleanor Tilney, "only put on a white gown; Miss Tilney always wears white". Austen uses white muslin to show the developing relationship between Catherine Morland and Henry Tilney, a man sensitive in his knowledge of muslins. "My sister has often trusted me in the choice of a gown," he says. "I bought one for her the other day, and it was pronounced to be a prodigious bargain by every lady who saw it. I gave but five shillings a yard for it, and a true Indian muslin."

The fashion for white gowns was imported from France in the 1780s into Britain and became the main mode of dress for women of all classes for several decades. These simple gowns were spiked with political significance in France, but in Britain they offered comfort and freedom, particularly when worn with flat slippers.

Britain was at war with France, revolution was in the air, and the flowing silhouette of women's dress referenced ancient Greece – and its art, democracy and enlightenment. The willowy, delicate silhouette was like that of a classical statue, while the crisp purity of white muslin, cambric or lawn fabric reinforced a sense of cleanliness in the age of the Industrial Revolution. White not only represented virtue, but it was elegant and delicate, suiting the Romantic vision of enlightenment.

Natural beauty was considered superior to the artifice of heavily adorned and padded gowns, and the precarious wigs toppling on heads. The white dress was both a luxury item and a symbol of the humble countryside worker; it was innocent in its use of white and also revealing, suggesting sexual promiscuity.

By the mid 1790s, the waistline rose to the bust, and little puffed sleeves were also introduced. These light, white gowns were showcased in influential British society magazine *La Belle Assemblée*, first published by John Bell in 1806. The 1 July 1806 issue depicted two ladies in flowing empire-waisted opera gowns of white India muslin, worn with white satin gloves and shoes. Another fashion plate showcased more modest white muslin walking dresses for taking a turn in Kensington Gardens, demonstrating their versatility.

As Britain took a foothold in India, the British East India Company began importing white Indian muslin, which was a much sought-after commodity for its fine translucence, with a texture as light as foam. In the eighteenth century, over half of the company's sales in London were of Indian textiles. Dhaka muslin from Bengal was the most prized. It was traded by Arab merchants throughout the Roman Empire from the first century CE, and made its way across Asia and into Europe when the Silk Road opened up. Yuan Chwang, a Chinese explorer to India in the seventh century CE, described the cloth as "like the light vapours of dawn".

Dhaka muslin was created from cotton that only grew on the banks of the Meghna River and, through a secret 16-step process, was hand-spun and woven into a fabric that was so delicate and wispy that its thread count was up to 1,200. India's Mughal rulers held this textile, and the skilled weavers, in high regard, but with the end of the Mughal empire, and the takeover of the subcontinent by the British Crown in the nineteenth century, the muslin industry was obliterated. The British East India Company, which wanted to sell its own imported cotton, pressured weavers into producing greater volumes of fabric at a lower cost, until they were pushed into ruin. By the beginning of the twentieth century, the complex weaving technique had been lost in time.

The beauty and romance of these delicate white fabrics hid the true horrors of colonialism, slavery and the exploitation of workers in the textile industry. At the end of the eighteenth century, mills across northern England sprang up to meet the demand for a home-produced muslin fabric. These mills not only depended on poorly paid and harshly treated workers, but also on American cotton, which was shipped from the burgeoning slave plantations in the southern states of America. Between 1619 and 1808, around 400,000 men and women were exported from Africa to America to pick and process the crop on the fertile lands of southern states like Mississippi.

While slaves were instrumental in providing cotton for white fashion fabrics, they were personally limited to the most basic fabrics, such as a White Welsh plains, a rough woollen cloth imported from Britain, which was referred to as "Negro cloth". In Shane White and Graham White's book *Stylin'* (1998), they noted that many of the runaway slaves taken to the workhouse in Charleston, South Carolina after being captured were listed as wearing this fabric. In 1765, two slaves were described as wearing "an old white negro cloth jacket and trowsers". A slave woman called Rhoad, who was reported missing in Frederick County, Maryland, in 1775 wore a white gown and "other clothing such as is common for slaves".

Many slaves rejected this rough white clothing and its symbolism of enslavement, choosing to create their own aesthetics, which would help in their escape and make them appear as free men. Some slaves also used their skills from working with textiles to dye their plain white clothing with cultivated indigo, and their botanical knowledge to create brown dye from walnut bark or yellow from cedar moss. By using different coloured dyes, slaves could create their own unique styles, such as adding patches to mend worn clothes, or applying coloured thread through woven material to create pretty dresses to wear on Sundays. In 1930, a former slave from Georgia named Benjamin Johnson told an interviewer for the Federal Writers' Project, which aimed to record narratives of those who had been enslaved, that while they wore "ol' plain white cloth", some was "patched so till dey looked like a quilt". What they adopted, according to the authors of *Stylin'*, "was an African American aesthetic, the use not only of varied materials and patterns but also of contrasting colors in a manner that jangled white sensibilities ... African textile traditions, handed down and adapted by African American women, that helped to shape the appearance of the antebellum slave community."

White weddings

When we think of white clothing, the first thing that is likely to come to mind is a wedding dress – a confection of frills and lace worn by a bride to traditionally signal her virginity and innocence on her wedding day. It's an old-fashioned notion that has less and less relevance in modern society, and despite these symbolic associations, what made white so cherished was its expense. The wedding gown is likely to be one of the costliest items of clothing a bride ever buys: a one-off piece of clothing that requires special care because of its colour and the delicate silks, satin and lace it contains.

After Queen Victoria married Prince Albert in an ivory satin wedding gown in 1840, she heralded a new custom for brides to wear white. Eighteenth-century fashion illustrations depicted wedding gowns in vivid red or other bright colours, while royal brides like Marie Antoinette and Princess Charlotte (when she married George III) preferred the prized metallic-threaded cloths.

While it wasn't a unique choice to wear white, with brides having done so before, the simplicity of Victoria's satin and lace was a contrast to the silver and gold splendour of previous queens. Agnes Strickland, in her biography of Victoria in 1840, wrote that the monarch was dressed "not as a queen in her glittering trappings, but in spotless white, like a pure virgin, to meet her bridegroom." But rather than it being a purposeful design to emphasize her virginity, she chose white as the perfect colour to promote the specially commissioned Honiton lace, made in Devon, on her gown, and as well as boosting the flagging lace industry, she made white a popular colour for wealthy brides.

Despite this, white gowns weren't practical, or affordable, for the average woman. As well as the cost of keeping white fabric pristine, not many could afford to purchase a gown that would be worn only once. Rather, they would choose a gown that could be reused for other occasions. This made white wedding dresses a desirable, but often out-of-reach, luxury in the nineteenth century.

The white of dreams and death

In many cultures, white symbolizes death and the afterlife. White is the Chinese colour of death and mourning, and was reserved for funerals during ancient dynasties. In Hindu tradition, widows are shrouded in white cloth. Vrindavan, near Delhi, is known as "the city of widows" because it attracts thousands of women covered in white cloth, most of whom are elderly, and have been sent away from their families following the death of their husbands.

With white representing both death and the celestial, ghosts came to be depicted in white gowns in Gothic art and literature. Romantic depictions often show us death after dark, the newly dead likely to be dressed in their white nightgowns, with their clothing crossing over with them into the afterlife.

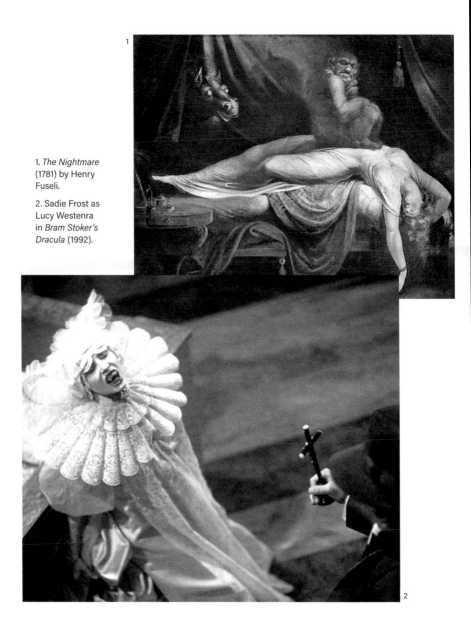

1. *The Nightmare* (1781) by Henry Fuseli.

2. Sadie Frost as Lucy Westenra in *Bram Stoker's Dracula* (1992).

One of the most influential Gothic images depicting a ghostly white neoclassical nightgown is in Henry Fuseli's 1781 painting *The Nightmare*. The Tate describes it as an "icon of horror"; the artist aimed to shock and intrigue with his depiction of a woman who appears to be hovering between deep sleep and death, in ecstasy or having fainted from desire, while an imp rests on her chest and a horse looks on. Perhaps it represents her nightmares, or it's an allegory of her sexuality, but from this painting, the idea of a woman in a white dress became a symbol of death and repressed desire. In Ken Russell's *Gothic* (1986), the director amped up the erotic charge of the Fuseli painting, with Natasha Richardson as Mary Shelley draped on a bed in a slinky white negligee as an incubus hovers over her.

In Gothic horror movies, female victims and vampires often wear stark white gowns, as with the character of Lucy in *Bram Stoker's Dracula* (1992). Not only do these replicate the notion of Fuseli's painting, of being spirited away, but the white represents both virginity and the white of traditional burial clothes.

Wilkie Collins's *The Woman in White* is considered the earliest example of the sensational suspense novel. Published in serial form in 1859, it thrilled its readers from the opening scene: Walter Hartright, an art teacher, is walking back to London late at night on a deserted road when the sensation of a hand on his shoulder sends a terrifying chill through him. He turns to see "the figure of a solitary Woman, dressed from head to toe in white garments". Not only is it odd that a woman should be out on the streets on her own, but her all-white outfit of dress and bonnet is considered unsuitable for wearing on the streets at night. The woman, Anne Catherick, has escaped from a lunatic asylum, and the white gown becomes a symbol of her mental instability as it is revealed that she chose only to wear white following a traumatic childhood.

White as a memory of the past is also referenced in interpretations of Emily Brontë's 1847 novel *Wuthering Heights*, as the costume of Catherine Earnshaw's spirit after she dies. In Kate Bush's music video for her 1978 hit 'Wuthering Heights', her ode to the Gothic novel, the ghostly white Victorian-style nightgown enhances her ethereal, exaggerated movements. Despite, or because of, the video's simplicity, she creates a powerful image through theatrical staging and choreography. The white dress helps her take on the spirit of Cathy, calling out to Heathcliff outside his window. It's witchy and mesmerizing, and reinforced the Gothic concept of the woman in white, hovering between both life and death.

There is also the character of Miss Havisham in Charles Dickens's *Great Expectations* (1860–1861), who is placed in unmarried limbo, still wearing the white wedding dress from when she was jilted by her lover. The decaying white gown keeps her in a position where she is neither living nor dead. Dickens wrote:

> She was dressed in rich materials, – satins, and lace, and silks, – all of white. Her shoes were white. And she had a long white veil dependent from her hair, and she had bridal flowers in her hair, but her hair was white ... I saw that everything within my view which ought to be white, had been white long ago, and had lost its lustre and was faded and yellow. I saw that the bride within the bridal dress had withered like the dress, and like the flowers, and had no brightness left but the brightness of her sunken eyes.

White satin on the silver screen
The concept of white as the colour of youth and of seduction would sweep the world following the Wall Street crash in 1929. The 1930s was an era Coco Chanel described

1. Lana Turner in *The Postman Always Rings Twice* (1946).

2. George Hurrell's portrait of Jean Harlow, circa 1934.

1

2

Alexandria Ocasio-Cortez and other Democratic representatives at the State of the Union, February 2019.

as "candid innocence and white satin", and she set trends with her romantic organdie gowns and white satin beach pyjamas. But it was in Hollywood that the white satin gown found its home, shimmering effectively on black and white film, and offering luxury, seduction and glamour as pure escapism for those who had been laid off work or who stood in breadlines as a result of the Great Depression.

The star who was most connected to white satin was the original blonde bombshell, Jean Harlow. MGM's costume designer Gilbert Adrian helped to shape this goddess image when he dressed her in pure white for films including *Bombshell* and *Dinner at Eight* (both 1933). In one famous promotional image, she reclined on a polar bear rug, dressed in white chiffon. Her high-maintenance white gowns represented purity and innocence, despite the brazen sex appeal for which she was famed. "White satin is sophisticated. So is the blondest of blondes, Jean Harlow. Together they are a glamorous picture," wrote *Movie Classic* magazine in December 1935.

While black was a recognizable code for a villain or a vamp, white typically represented goodness. Yet Lana Turner's costumes in *The Postman Always Rings Twice* (1946) turned this convention on its head. For the femme fatale to wear pristine white throughout the movie was unexpected, and adds to the complexity of the character of Cora Smith, whose hot and heavy affair with John Garfield's drifter, Frank Chambers, leads to sadomasochism and murder. As the director Tay Garnett said: "The white clothing was something that Carey [Wilson, producer] and I thought of. At that time there was a great problem getting a story with that much sex past the censors. We figured that dressing Lana in white somehow made everything she did seem less sensuous. It was also attractive as hell." In her retrospective review of the film, Pauline Kael, film critic at *The New Yorker*, noted that Lana as Cora was dressed "in impeccable white, as if to conceal her sweaty passions and murderous impulses".

The white pantsuit

When New York Democratic congresswoman Alexandria Ocasio-Cortez was sworn into office in January 2019, she purposefully chose to wear a white trouser suit. Adopting the colour as a link to the suffragettes who achieved votes for women a century before, she announced on Instagram that it was "in honour of the women who came before me, and the women yet to come".

The colour white, along with purple and green, was chosen by Emmeline Pethick-Lawrence to unify Britain's Suffragette movement, which had seen 300,000 women turn out to London's Hyde Park in 1908 to protest the right for women to vote. In America, the suffragettes combined white with gold and purple, to similarly symbolize their purity and virtue. As the movement gained popularity in both the United States and Britain, wearing a touch of white was a simple way to show allegiance to the cause. Choosing feminine white clothing was also a way for the suffragettes to avoid the common trope of being labelled "manly", so that their protests would be heard.

White was later picked up by women in American politics as a colour that symbolizes empowerment and new beginnings. In 1969, Shirley Chisholm wore an all-white outfit after being elected as the first black woman into the United States Congress, and Geraldine Ferraro wore a white suit when she accepted her nomination as the first female vice president in 1984.

Hillary Clinton was known for her love of a white pantsuit, wearing a Ralph Lauren version at the Democratic National Convention in summer 2016, and another for the third presidential debate in October 2016. There was a surge in interest in white pantsuits on the back of these appearances. Katherine Ormerod, editorial director for global e-commerce platform Lyst, was quoted in the *New York Times* as saying: "The pantsuit has had a massive resurgence in interest with a 460 percent uplift since

January 2016. The interest in white pantsuits in particular has certainly confounded expectations – especially as we usually see a seasonal dip for white color ways across every category."

In the lead-up to the 2016 election, a grassroots campaign hashtag urged women to #WearWhiteToVote, as a way of paying tribute to the suffragettes. Clinton poignantly wore another Ralph Lauren white pantsuit with matching wool coat at the inauguration of President Trump in January 2017, as a symbol of hope and courage in defeat following election loss, and, in her own words, "to honour our democracy".

When Melania Trump wore an ivory Christian Dior pantsuit to the State of the Union address in 2018, the first time she had appeared in public to support her husband following the scandal of Donald Trump's affair with adult film star Stormy Daniels, her choice of colour raised eyebrows. Melania Trump's wardrobe was often coded, such as wearing a pink pussy-bow blouse following her husband's *Access Hollywood* scandal, or a jacket controversially emblazoned with the words "I don't care, do you?" Perhaps she was deliberately provoking female Democrats by wearing the colour they had adopted, or in a reading that many Democratic women preferred, maybe she was offering a feminist rebuke to her husband for his numerous affairs.

Minimalism and futurism
When people imagined the future in the 1960s, at the advent of the Space Age, it was typically envisioned in white and silver – clinical, clean and sleek. This was the colour of the NASA-designed space suits for sending astronauts into space, and of the white and silver dresses constructed from metal and plastics by designers André Courrèges and Paco Rabanne. André Courrèges admired the cleanliness of white, which reminded him of tennis

clothing and the limewash of Spanish houses, and he invented his own bleach with a blueing agent to make it even more brilliant white. His white tunics, mini-skirts, go-go boots and helmets defined the style of his "Moon Girls" from his 1965 collection, who wouldn't have looked out of place on the set of Stanley Kubrick's *2001: A Space Odyssey*, released only a few years later, in 1968. As Susan Train, fashion editor of American *Vogue*, recollected of this ground-breaking collection: "The skirts were short compared with those of other designers. They got everyone into tunics and pants, and there was lots of white, which was such a shock."

Over the last few decades, white has been embraced as part of the fashion for minimalism, from Calvin Klein's unisex underwear to Apple's iPhone products, where white is imbued with traditional notions of purity, cleanliness and exclusivity. A white T-shirt, like that of actor James Dean, or Kate Moss in Calvin Klein's 1990s ads, is misleading in its unpretentiousness, as it is the ultimate in casual, yet deliberate, style.

In 1996, Tom Ford, as Creative Director of Gucci, sent models like Kirsty Hume and Carolyn Murphy down the runway in a minimalist white gown with a keyhole at the hip, revealing a glimpse of flesh and no underwear underneath. The dress, which sold out almost immediately, entirely encapsulated the symbolism of white – simplicity, high-maintenance, luxurious and innocent, with the underlying hint of simmering sexuality under the cool surface.

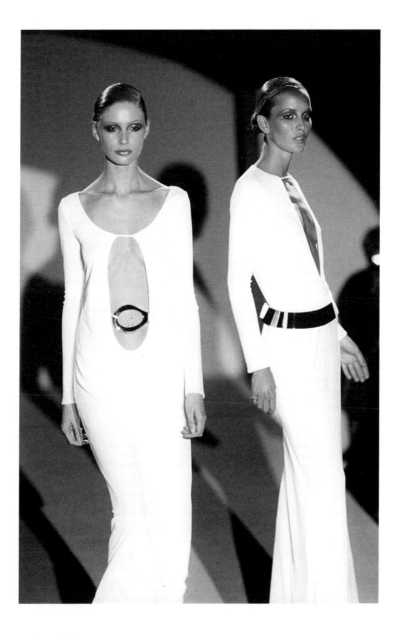

Tom Ford for
Gucci, A/W
1996.

Selected Bibliography

Capote, T. (1998). *Breakfast at Tiffany's*. London: Penguin.

Chitnis, C. (2020). *Patterns of India: A Journey Through Colors, Textiles, and the Vibrancy of Rajasthan*. New York: Pisces Books.

Chrisman-Campbell, K. (2015). *Fashion Victims: Dress at the Court of Louis XVI and Marie-Antoinette*. London: Yale University Press.

Dean, J. (2018). *Wild Colour: How to Make and Use Natural Dyes*. London: Mitchell Beazley.

Downing, S. (2010). *Fashion in the Time of Jane Austen*. London: Shire Library.

Phipps, E. (2010). *Cochineal Red: The Art History of a Color*. New York: Metropolitan Museum of Art.

Evans, G. (2017). *The Story of Colour: An Exploration of the Hidden Messages of the Spectrum*. London: Michael O'Mara.

Fox, C. (2018). *Vogue Essentials: Little Black Dress*. London: Conran.

Fraser, A. (2002). *Marie Antoinette*. London: Weidenfeld and Nicolson.

Garfield, S. (2018). *Mauve: How one man invented a colour that changed the world*. London: Canongate.

Goodman, R. (2017). *How to be a Tudor: A Dawn-to-Dusk Guide to Everyday Life.* New York: Liveright.

Goodwin, J. (2003). *A Dyer's Manual*. London: Ashmans Publications.

Jaeger, Gustav, trans. Tomalin, Lewis RS. (1887) *Dr Jaeger's Essays on Health-Culture.* London: Waterlow and Sons.

Kobal, J. (1977). *Rita Hayworth: The Time, the Place, the Woman.* London: WH Allen.

Laverty, C. (2021). *Fashion in Film*. London: Laurence King.

Luhanko, D. and Neumuller, K. (2018). *Indigo: Cultivate, Dye, Create*. London: Pavilion.

Lynn, E. (2017). *Tudor Fashion*. Connecticut: Yale University Press.

Matthews David, A. (2017). *Fashion Victims: The Dangers of Dress Past and Present*. London: Bloomsbury Visual Arts.

McDonald, F. (2012). *Textiles: A History*. Yorkshire: Pen & Sword.

McKinley, C. (2011). *Indigo: In Search of the Colour that Seduced the World*. London: Bloomsbury.

Paoletti, J.B. (2002*) Pink and Blue: Telling the Boys and Girls in America*. Indiana: Indiana University Press.

Pastoureau, M. (2017). *Red: The History of a Color*. New Jersey: Princeton University Press.

Perrault, C. (2019). *The Fairy Tales of Charles Perrault: with original color illustrations by Harry Clarke*. Ballingslöv: Wisehouse Publishing.

Petherbridge, D. (2013). *Witches and Wicked Bodies*. Edinburgh: National Galleries of Scotland in association with the British Museum.

Pliny the Elder. (1991). *The Natural History*, Book 20, Chap.79. London: Penguin Classics.

Postrel, V. (2020). *The Fabric of Civilization: How Textiles Made the World*. New York: Basic Books.

Robinson, S. (1969). *A History of Dyed Textiles*. London: Studio Vista London.

Schiaparelli, E. (2007). *Shocking Life: The Autobiography of Elsa Schiaparelli*. London: V&A Fashion Perspectives.

Shrimpton, J. (2016). *Victorian Fashion*. Oxford: Shire.

St Clair, K. (2019). *The Golden Thread: How Fabric Changed History*. London: John Murray.

St Clair, K. (2016). *The Secret Lives of Colour*. London: John Murray.

Steele, V. (2008). *Gothic: Dark Glamour*. Connecticut: Yale University Press.

Steele, V. (2018). *Pink: The History of a Punk, Pretty, Powerful Color*. New York: Thames and Hudson.

Strickland, A. (1840). *Queen Victoria from her birth to her bridal: In two volumes*. London: Henry Colbern.

Truhler, K. (2020). *Film Noir Style: The Killer 1940s*. Pittsburgh: GoodKnight Books.

Vigée-Lebrun, L., trans. Strachey, L. (1903) *Memoirs of Madame Vigée Lebrun*. New York: Doubleday, Page & Company.

White, S. and White, G. (1998). *Stylin': African American Expressive Culture From Its Beginnings to the Zoot Suit*. New York: Cornell University Press.

Journals

Bryant, K.N. (Fall 2015). *The making of a western-negro-superhero-savior: Django's blue velvet Fauntleroy suit*. Studies in Popular Culture, Vol. 38, No. 1.

Guéguen, N., and Jacob, C. (2012). *Lipstick and tipping behavior: when red lipstick enhances waitresses' tips*. International Journal of Hospitality Management, Vol. 31.

Jack, B. (April 30, 2014). *Goethe's Werther and its effects*. The Lancet.

Lubrich, N. (December 2015). *The Wandering Hat: Iterations of the medieval Jewish pointed cap*. Jewish History, Vol. 29, No. 3/4.

Nicklas, C.C. (November 2009). *Splendid Hues: Colour, Dyes, Everyday Science, and Women's Fashion, 1840 - 1875*. University of Brighton.

Niesta-Kayser, D., Elliot, A.J. and Feltman, R. (2010). *Red and romantic behavior in men viewing women*, European Journal of Social Psychology, Vol. 40.

Sukenik, N., Iluz, D., Amar, Z., Varvak, A., Workman, V., Shamir, O., and Ben-Yosef, E. (June 28, 2017). *Early evidence (late 2nd millennium BCE) of plant-based dyeing of textiles from Timna, Israel*. Plos One

Worth, R. (September 13, 2013). *Clothing in the Landscape: Change and the Rural Vision in the Work of Thomas Hardy (1840 to 1928)*. Cambridge University Press.

Newspapers and magazines

AnOther Mag. (4 January 2019). 'How Wearing White Became a Symbol of Female Solidarity.'

Associated Press. (1 September 2017). 'Prince's Other Sister confirms What We've Known all Along.'

The Atlantic, Zafar, A. (15 March 2010). *Deconstructing Lady Gaga's 'Telephone' Video.*

BBC Future, Gorvett, Z. (17 March 2021). 'The Legendary Fabric that No One Knows How to Make.'

The Cut, Hyland, V. (2 August 2016). 'Why Is Millennial Pink Suddenly So Popular?'

Glamour Magazine, Lester, T.L. (10 October 2011). 'A real Life Pan Am Stewardess on What It Was Like to Wear That Famous Uniform.'

Guardian, Cartner-Morley, J. (10 June 2015). 'Elizabeth Hurley at 50: How She Has Influenced your Wardrobe (whether you like it or not).'

Guardian, Cocozza, P. (20 May 2010). 'Nude: is the hot fashion colour racist?'

Guardian, Cartner-Morley, J. (26 July 2017) 'Club Tropicana! Why kitsch is everywhere this summer.'

JSTOR Daily, Brennan, S. (9 September 2017). 'A Natural History of the Wedding Dress.'

Life. (18 August 1961). 'Four Lovelies Express Themselves in Color on A Daffy Tinge Binge.'

New York Times, Robertson, N.C. (22 May 1963). 'Set the Trends in Living for Many Other Americans.'

New York Times. (23 July 1893). 'Finery for Infants.'

New York Times, Emerson, G. (10 July 1958). 'Jeans Resist Any Change in 108 Years'

New York Times, Espen, H. (21 March 1999). 'Levi's Blues.'

New York Times, Friedman, V. (30 January 2018). 'Melania Trump and the Case of the White Pantsuit.'

New York Times, Friedman, V. (7 November 2016). 'On Election Day, the Hillary Clinton White Suit Effect.'

New York Times. (6 April 1959). 'Pink is Pushed as Fashion Hue.'

New York Times, Elder, R. (28 October 1973). 'Retain Chic in London.'

New York Times, Holmes, C. (16 November 1952). 'This is the Beat Generation.'

Nylon, Soo Hoo, F. (2 July 2020). 'Why the Yellow Dress Will Forever be Iconic, from Rom-Coms to Fairy Tales.'

Photoplay, Scullin, G. (November 1956). 'The Girl with the Lavender life.'

Stylist, Wills, K. (15 October 2016). 'Aubergine is the new black: from lips to chips the eggplant is having a cultural moment right now.'

The Times, Hulanicki, B. (August 15, 1983). 'The Dedicated Modeller of Fashion.'

The Times. (1 December 1803). 'London Fashions for December.'

Vogue Business, Maguire, L. (26 October 2020). 'Kim Kardashian: On Shapewear.'

Credits

The publishers would like to thank the following sources for their kind permission to reproduce the pictures in this book.

Alamy: AA Film Archive 150 (bottom left), 202 (right); /AF Archive 172 (bottom left), 191 (bottom); /Alain Le Garsmeur London, 1972 54; /Album 157 (top right), 219 (bottom); /Allstar Picture Library Ltd 83 (centre); /Hendrik Ballhausen/dpa 147 (right); /Collection Christop168 (bottom left); /Collection Christophel 105 (bottom); /Cineclassico 208 (bottom), 245 (bottom); /Ian Dagnall Computing 232 (left), 242 (top); /Everett Collection Inc 106; /History and Art Collection (top) 184; /Incamerastock 196 (bottom); /Moviestore Collection Ltd 126 (centre); /Landmark Media Lebrecht Music & Arts 184 (bottom left); /Painters 90 (top left); /Photo12 176 (top right); /PictureLux/The Hollywood Archive 132 (top); /Retro AdArchives 163 (top right); /Science History Images 140

Bridgeman Images: Copyright DACS 2021 96 (top)

Getty Images: AFP 150 (top left); /Don Arnold/WireImage 72 (bottom); /Art Images 140 (top); /Art Media/Print Collector 67 (top); /Toni Anne Barson/WireImage 196 (top); /Edward Berthelot 173 (bottom right); /Bettmann 83 (bottom); /Antonio de Moraes Barros Filho/WireImage 133, 220 (top right); /Edward Berthelot 6; /Bettmann 30 top; /Corbis News 227; /Estrop 202; /Giuseppe Cacace/AFP 84 (right); /Stephane Cardinale/Corbis 203 (right); /Jean Chung 132; /James Devaney/WireImage 122 (bottom); /Dia Dipasupil 226 (left); /Ed Feingersh/Michael Ochs Archives 30 c; /David Fenton 20 top; / Fine Art Images/Heritage Images 184 (right) /Fox Photos/Hulton Archive 77 (bottom); /Ron Galella, Ltd./Ron Galella Collection 168 (bottom); /Lynn Goldsmith 10; /Steve Grayson/WireImage for BET Entertainment 56 (top); /Francois Guillot/AFP 220 (bottom); /Heritage Art/Heritage Images 90 (top right), 162 (top left); /Hulton Archive 76 (centre); /Anwar Hussein/WireImage 163 (bottom); /Chris Jackson 106; /Alain Jocard/AFP 56; /Dimitrios Kambouris 115 (bottom); /George Karger 223; /Jeff Kravitz/FilmMagic, Inc 115 (top right); /Jackson Lee/GC Images 156 (bottom); /Leemage/Corbis 115 (top left); /Francis G. Mayer/Corbis/VCG 20 bottom; /Kevin Mazur/Getty Images 109 (top), 223 (top); /Arik McArthur/WireImage 77 (top); /Museum of London/Heritage Images 51 (top right); /Photo 12 61; /PictureLux/The Hollywood Archive 245 (top); /Popperfoto 168 (top); /The Print Collector 208 (top right); /PYMCA/Universal Images Group 30 bottom; /Rolls Press/Popperfoto 51 (bottom); /Pascal Le Segretain 150 (top right), 220 (top left); /Silver Screen Collection 123 (top), 172 (top); /Brendan Smialowski 176 (bottom); /SSPL 97 (bottom); /Sunset Boulevard/Corbis 51 (top left), 236; /Universal History Archive/Universal Images Group 147 (top left); /VCG Wilson/Corbis 90 (bottom); /Justin de Villeneuve/Hulton Archive

54 (top); /Victor Virgile/Gamma-Rapho 109 (bottom), 133 (top left), 133 (top right), 150 (bottom right), 226 (left); /Peter White 84 (left); /Patrick De Wilde/Gamma-Rapho 67 (bottom); /Vittorio Zunino Celotto/Getty Images for LuisaViaRoma 31

New York Public Library: Copyright photograph by Diana Davies 54 (centre)

Public Domain: 232 (top)

Shutterstock: 232 (right); /Alex Bailey/Focus Features/Kobal 100 (top); / Matt Baron 82 (top), 122 (centre); /Columbia/Kobal 137; /Columbia/The Weinstein Company/Kobal 72; /Faherty/Mgm/Kobal 191 (top); /Howell Conant/Paramount/Kobal 21; /Everett Collection 100 (bottom); /Kharbine-Tapabor 208 (top left); /Mgm/Kobal 105 (top); /Moviestore 126 (top), 137 (top), 219 (top); /Dale Robinette/Black Label Media/Kobal 126 (bottom); / SIPA 176 (top left); /Snap 203 (left), 242 (bottom); /Alberto Terenghi/IP 156 (top left); /Shawn Thew/EPA-EFE 246; /Ken Towner/ANL 251; /Warner Bros/Kobal 41

Every effort has been made to acknowledge correctly and contact the source and/or copyright holder of each picture and Welbeck Non-fiction Limited apologizes for any unintentional errors or omissions, which will be corrected in future editions of this book.

Author acknowledgements

I'm grateful to my agent Isabel Atherton at Creative Authors, who I'm very happy to have on my side. Thanks also to Isabel Wilkinson at Welbeck for being so enthusiastic and helping me shape the idea, and to Emily Voller, Ocky Murray and Katie Baxendale for creating the beautiful design of this book.

Cover design: Emily Voller
Spread design: Ocky Murray
Art direction: Katie Baxendale
Editorial: Isabel Wilkinson and Millie Acers
Production: Marion Storz
Picture research: Steve Behan